JAMES L. CHRISTENSEN, Senior Minister of
Lindenwood Christian Church, Memphis,
Tennessee, is a graduate of the Seminary of
Phillips University. He has received numer-
ous honors for his speaking and writing
activities and is considered an authority
among ministers. He is the author of THE
COMPLETE FUNERAL MANUAL, FU-
NERAL SERVICES, THE MINISTER'S
MARRIAGE HANDBOOK, THE MINIS-
TER'S SERVICE HANDBOOK and CON-
TEMPORARY WORSHIP SERVICES.

NEW WAYS
TO WORSHIP

BY *James L. Christensen*

NEW WAYS
TO WORSHIP

More Contemporary Worship Services

JAMES L. CHRISTENSEN

FLEMING H. REVELL COMPANY

Old Tappan, New Jersey

Library of Congress Cataloging in Publication Data

Christensen, James L
   New ways to worship.

   Bibliography: p.
   1. Worship programs. I. Title.
BV198.C54   264   73–933
ISBN 0–8007–0583–1

ACKNOWLEDGMENTS

Excerpts from *A Complete Funeral Manual* by James L. Christensen, © copyright 1967, published by Fleming H. Revell Company, are used by permission.

"Ain't Gonna Study War No More," adaptation by Jack Fascinato and Ernest J. Ford © 1960 Snyder Music Corporation is used by permission.

"Genesis—Last Chapter" by Kenneth Ross is from *The Conservationist* (June–July, 1971 issue) published by the New York State Department of Environmental Conservation and is used by permission.

"The Influence of One Life" is adapted from the scroll in The Garden at Clifton's, Los Angeles, California. Copyright 1955, by Christian Board of Publication. Used by permission.

Excerpt from ARE YOU RUNNING WITH ME, JESUS? by Malcolm Boyd. Copyright © 1965 by Malcolm Boyd. Reprinted by permission of Holt, Rinehart and Winston, Inc.

Selections from *Interrobang* by Norman C. Habel, published by Fortress Press are reprinted by permission.

Selections from *And God Wants People* by Mary Lou Lacy. © M. E. Bratcher 1962. Used by permission of John Knox Press.

Excerpt from *New Forms of Worship* by James F. White, published by Abingdon Press is used by permission.

"Confession for Misuse of Earth" by Jack W. Lundin is from LITURGIES FOR LIFE, reprinted by permission of the CCS Publishing House, Box 107, Downers Grove, Illinois 60615.

Selection from MORE CONTEMPORARY PRAYERS edited by Caryl Micklem is published by Wm. B. Eerdmans in the United States and by SCM Press, Ltd. in the United Kingdom. Used by permission.

Selection from THE BOOK OF WORSHIP FOR CHURCH AND HOME © 1964, 1965, by the Board of Publication of the Methodist Church, Inc. is used by permission.

Selection from THE FREEDOM SEDER by Arthur I. Waskow. Copyright © 1969, 1970 by The Religious Community of Micah. Reprinted by permission of Holt, Rinehart and Winston, Inc.

CONTENTS

INTRODUCTION

The love for God is expressed in many ways. I have shared in a variety of worship services—from the stately formal procedures of a cathedral mass to the informal worship of a conference in the Rocky Mountains. I have worshiped with the majestic sounds of a fifty-bank, four-keyboard pipe organ and hundred-voice choir, as well as with the strums of a guitar and the blare of "holy rock"—or, frequently, with no instruments at all. I have worshiped in the high church of the Anglicans as well as the informal emotionally charged services of the Pentecostals and Southern Baptists. My heart has been warmed and God praised in each form.

Much of the efficacy of worship depends on the worshiper and his particular preparation. What to me is worshipful, inspirational, and a worthy offering to God, may seem lifeless and inappropriate to others. What is appreciated by the older folks may be far different from what the younger people desire. Often youth use new ways of expressing their religious beliefs and feelings.

Some of the newer ways of worship may be startling. The folk music, snapping of fingers, clapping of hands, informal atmosphere, balloons, lend spirit to the young in their own mod way— yet to others—especially the older generation—it is offensive and out of character. Yet, some of these so-called newer ways are a recovering of old ways that used to be widespread.

However, to be Christian, worship must be set in the midst of Christian tradition, so that it has integrity. Worship is Christian if it enables the worshiper to grasp what God did in Christ. The basic ingredients of the service must reflect the theological

11

structure depicting new life in Christ. Once that theological basis is adequately included, then the leader is free to include varied contemporary artistic, cultural, and verbal material.

Worship is celebration, but not all celebration is worship. Christian worship celebrates what God has done in Christ, which gives hope, new life, community—reasons for celebration even in the midst of life's sordid circumstances.

It is impossible, therefore, to prescribe precise materials and forms for everyone or every group. Our cultural, intellectual, fellowship, and emotional orientation are so varied. Each in his own tongue and each in his own way is the freedom accorded Christ's flock. This book, however, is an aid for new forms of contemporary worship. It is my contention that every church should inculcate some innovative services to give freshness and aliveness to worship.

The idea of this book is not to give you a package which you can apply to your unique circumstance. Rather, it is a resource from which you can receive suggestions to develop your own service. This book indicates what some varied worshiping communities have experienced.

I want to express my great debt to many minister friends who have shared material and have encouraged me in this project, and to my wife, Margaret, who has shared her voluminous reading gems, given advice, and read and corrected the manuscript. My sincere thanks go to my secretary, Nancee Zidnak, whose organized, efficient preparation of the manuscript has made the book possible.

Section 1

DEVELOPING THE CONTEMPORARY ATMOSPHERE

Section 1

DEVELOPING THE CONTEMPORARY ATMOSPHERE

MARKS OF CONTEMPORARY WORSHIP

The contemporary worship service is a phenonemon of the last ten years. It has emerged at a time when the American church has been in decline and increasingly sterile. To recover its mission and influence, the church has attempted to become more relevant and vital. A Holy-Spirit emphasis has characterized many churches reacting to the antiemotionalism period; sacramental renewal has emerged to compensate for the liturgical decline of the revivalism period; experimental worship with flexibility and spontaneity is increasingly used to complement or replace the more rigid, formal traditional services.

Experimental worship is generally characterized by five marks. The first is a *participational style*. Worship is not something observed or attended; it is something we *do*. Involvement of the worshipers in singing, movement, reading, antiphonal chants, and every innovative way is felt to be desirable. Worship is more

14

than a professional cleric doing the ritual; it involves all who worship. It is not a performance put on for the members with the clergyman the star. In the traditional service, the effectiveness and vitality in shaping human beings depends on the abilities of the pastor and the professionalism of the choir.

Celebration is the overriding mood of contemporary worship. Its purpose is to convey the joy and enthusiasm that results from the good news of God's love. God is alive. God is love. Worship is not the funeral of a dead God; rather it is celebrating the exciting, exhilarating assurance of a living Lord who has vindicated love, righteousness, and hope. Contemporary worship strives to make the experience enjoyable and exciting to replace the dreary, dull, and sleepy experiences of much traditional worship.

Going to church to some has been like going to a movie, where one slips into a seat, possibly unnoticed and unknown by those about him, to privately view a performance on the chancel. Contemporary worship is a *communal gathering*. Great emphasis is placed on togetherness, touching, speaking—so that one's consciousness overlaps with others. It encourages close interpersonal relationships so that the worshiper looks at his neighbors, touches them, and may even talk to them. The family dimension is realized for "no man is an island." Corporate prayer, corporate speaking parts, worshiping as a congregation is basic in the new trend.

Likewise, contemporary worship attempts to recapture the dramatic *mystical* dimension of life. Today's society with its technical, scientific, and rational style has tended to rob people of the mysterious. The Now generation is hungry for the mystical experience indicated by the widespread interest in astrology, experimentation with drugs, extrasensory perception and the glossolalia movement. Whereas traditional worship is orderly, rational, and packaged, contemporary worship is more of an experience to be felt by all the senses. Whereas traditional worship follows a meticulously similiar order and pattern of worship Sunday-in and Sunday-out, contemporary worship leaves room for *variety* and *mobility*. Worshipers may well expect a different physical arrangement, procedure, style and type of content each

Sunday. (When too extreme, of course, this creates resistance.) The primary purpose is to get away from sameness by creative planning and utilization of different media.

SUGGESTIONS FOR CREATING THE CONTEMPORARY

What can we do to create a contemporary worship setting? What can the average minister of the average congregation do? It is a difficult assignment to avoid being foolishly innovative yet flexible and open to helpful expressions. Here are some suggestions that I hope are not too extreme which may stimulate possibilities:

Use a Fuller Range of Musical Instruments and Celebrative Songs Traditional worship has been accompanied quite largely by only the organ. To be sure the organ is a versatile, beautiful instrument. Most formal church services need the organ. We remain grateful for it and for those who play the instrument.

However, why not also organize an ensemble of guitars? or form an orchestra of a dozen instruments to play religious music? There is nothing like a blaring trumpet to create excitement and celebration, plus the steady beat of the drum.

Few worshipers feel celebration or joy in church music. Often it is dull, somber, and uninspiring—a poor offering to the Lord.

I believe in peppy, enthusiastic rhythm, in which all participate, occasionally accompanied with clapping, foot-tapping, or swaying. Perhaps your choir can be changed from the role of performer to that of enabler. Instead of being set apart from the congregation, why not have the choir on the same level with the congregation? Can the choir be located so that they lead and assist the worshipers in "singing to the Lord," as a part of the worshiping community, not as the performers? While a hymn is sung the choir might disperse throughout the sanctuary, moving about as they sing, encouraging congregational participation. Incidentally, while among the people, an excellent opportunity is afforded to symbolize community as the choir members transcend the aisles by joining hands with people on both sides of the aisle.

With the entire congregation holding hands, there is created a sense of oneness.

The choir or soloist may sing the verses of a song with the congregation joining in on the chorus. The trained choir gives the messages in song of the more complex and difficult type, not as entertainment for the worshipers, rather, on their behalf unto God.

Included in the music repertoire of the congregation should be some of the fine contemporary songs. Why are so many churches hung up on the old subjective gospel songs, yet are resistant to learning new contemporary music? The gospel hymn has a place in the church to be sure, yet many good hymns have been written in the last ten years which are not generally welcomed in the sanctuary. One example is, "Turn, Turn, Turn," written by Pete Seeger, and taken exclusively from Ecclesiastes, chapter 3. Perhaps you can organize in your church, youth singing groups with the contemporary sound to teach and lead the congregation.

Some of the recorded music of modern hymns could be played to familiarize the congregation and choir with the tunes and words.

Perhaps a place to begin is for the pastor to use some of the contemporary songs as prayers, confessions, readings. Many of the contemporary songs have been written by young people and express their concerns and theology.

Utilize Movement   Worship celebration involves not only the audio, verbal, and visual senses. It should involve the whole body. As Dr. James White indicates, "To move people spiritually, it is often necessary to move them physically." [1]

Opportunities for physical movement probably can be provided in your worship.

While singing a praise hymn, the congregation might be encouraged to stand, lift their hands in praise; or, as in the Billy Graham Crusades, to lift an arm with the index finger pointed up. During a more subdued mood, the congregation may sway in unison.

Marching is familiar to all of us, as a rallying type of movement for focusing political and social witness. It has been used
from ancient times in both Judaic and Christian worship. During
a rhythmic processional hymn, the choir may come down the
aisle, not so much in the precision, rigid, military march, but
rather gliding in a joyous type of movement. The choir may
divide at the front of the aisle, move to the side aisles to the
choir area. Modifications of this suggestion, of course, will be
necessary according to physical circumstances and congregational
cooperation.

A major procession involving the entire membership may be
accomplished on anniversary festival days. For example, on a
day such as Palm Sunday, the entire membership may meet at
the parking lot (or in an adjacent large room if weather requires) while a good brass ensemble with plenty of trumpets
plays joyous church hymns. At the appropriate time, the band
will lead the procession around the church building and into the
sanctuary, perhaps around the inside of the sanctuary. Worshipers form a double line. Each person is given a palm leaf to wave
recalling Jesus' entrance into Jerusalem. A person carrying a
cross might lead the procession. Banners can be scattered
throughout the marchers as well as placards with appropriate
words and symbols. Balloons and flowers will add excitement.
The marchers sing heartily and triumphantly. Such a movement
is not an every-Sunday possibility, and should be reserved only
for the celebration of very special observances.

People should enjoy their worship. So, during hymns they
should feel free to tap a foot, clap hands, or shout an *amen* as
an involvement.

An opportunity at the beginning of worship or preceding intercessory prayers should be given for worshipers to speak to,
touch, and talk with those around them. Many worshipers these
days see other worshipers only at church. Therefore, an opportunity for showing concern, touching one another and visiting is
desirable. An expressive act like an embrace, with the partici-

pants nodding their heads over one shoulder then the other, is one possibility of expressing community.

Kneeling is a posture expressing humility, encouraged during times of confession or of petition. Also, the gesture of beating one's chest, or a series of nodding expresses penitence before God. Arms stretched upward gestures a call for mercy.

Standing is the most appropriate posture for praise, or prayers of adoration and offering. Sitting is an appropriate posture for communion and for listening to the Scripture lessons and sermons.

A gesture indicating one's reconciliation with his neighbor is the passing of the peace. The peace is most often given with a double handclasp. The minister usually initiates the passing, by going to the first person in each pew, who in turn passes it down the aisle with the handshake or embrace saying, "The peace of the Lord be with you, _____ (*person's name*)," and the response, "And with your spirit." This may be done after prayers of confession, before the offering, at the conclusion of the Lord's Supper, or after the benediction. The embrace is the best symbolic gesture of reconciliation.

If the congregation is not large, the worshipers may take their offerings to the altar table as a token of total dedication. Otherwise representatives of the congregation receive the gifts to the Lord.

Likewise, for the Lord's Supper, the congregation may move to either stand or kneel about the table to receive the emblems of God's love.

Increasingly, it is felt that when possible worshipers should bring emblems themselves, to take to the table as their gifts to the common meal. The movement forward to the altar table has theological implications. People come forward to receive the benefits of Christ which the Lord's table symbolically makes available. Breaking pieces of bread from a common loaf symbolizes the "breaking." Worshipers serving each other the emblems emphasizes the *koinonia* dimension—the sharing of grace. Contemporary worship encourages close, interpersonal relationships so that persons look at their neighbors, talk to them, touch them, and serve them. Segments of the congregation in groups of twelve, twenty-five, or fifty may be taken to an adjacent room for sharing and communion to accomplish some of this.

Vary the Order and Content   The key factors in contemporary worship are flexibility and variety.

Worship is an awareness of being in the presence of God, and the response from that experience. The worshiper responds to this sense of God's nearness by making some worthy offering of adoration, praise, better understanding of God's will, and undertaking God's challenging mission to the world. Traditionally, a definite cycle of expression formed a routine pattern. It was the same for each worship occasion with four definite acts: reverence, fellowship, dedication, and renewal. These movements, in the liturgical setting, were carefully designed from a theological-psychological perspective. There are, to be sure, essential elements for worship to be worship. Not all celebration is worship. Not all gatherings can be construed as worship of God. Certainly, true worship should include praise, confession, thanksgiving, offering, intercession, the Word read and proclaimed, and the celebration of hope.

Without discrediting or contradicting the traditional theological motivations, contemporary worship at its best, deliberately utilizes variety.

However, to escape the monotony of sameness, and to give the possibility of fresh experiences, a constant reordering of procedure and placement of content is desirable. In keeping with the focus of the two great commandments, worship at times is pointed to God and the order of salvation—confession, assurance, nurture, and response. At other times it is directed to service in the secular world.

In contemporary worship, for example, a medley of songs (five or six) might be sung one after the other, expressing varied content: adoration, celebration, confession, assurance, dedication.

The anthem and sermon are placed in the order according to content. For example, if the theme is stewardship of money, the sermon should precede the offering opportunity in order to give a deeper significance to this important worship response. If the sermon is on confession, it should precede the prayers of confession. Likewise the sermon, if it is an exposition of the Word, should follow closely the reading of the Word.

There is nothing sacrosanct about communion at a particular location. Its placement depends upon the other content and emphasis of the service, which might be the conclusion, or the central focus, or conceivably at the beginning.

Contemporary worship services are usually planned around a particular theme. This planning may well involve the lay people, along with clergy, in determining goals, materials, and participants.

Themes may be selected around the liturgical Christian calendar, the secular calendar, Bible lectionary, Christian traditions, denominational emphases, topics, community experiences, and need.

There is a great variety of possibilities for involvement which the creative person will discover.

To vary procedures risks negative reactions from those steeped in wooden orthodoxy. Change is traumatic for some. Actually, for those who have a deep understanding and appreciation for the consistent liturgical order, there should be regular traditional services available. Some congregations are scheduling both a traditional and a contemporary service each week.

Personalize Prayers Prayers are integral to corporate worship. The church at worship is a worldwide centuries-long community that has a sense of the Holy God. It interprets life within that context. Prayer publicly affirms this common belief and lays open the concerns, hopes, and failures of the congregation.

However, much prayer has been too stilted, wordy, meticulously eloquent, and sermonic. Sometimes it sounds as if the one praying were attempting to impress the listeners with beautifully turned phrases. They merit Paul's verdict: "clanging cymbals."

The new attempt is to make prayer a heartfelt experience and expression to God by the entire congregation. Hence, efforts should be made for participation by the worshipers with spontaneous prayers, dialogue prayers, responsive litanies, etc. Such prayers are less beautiful, but more meaningful to the worshipers. Instead of the minister vocalizing on behalf of the worshipers their feelings to God, persons should have opportunities, individually and collectively, to "say their prayers."

One suggestion is to have *bidding prayers,* where the leader of worship suggests the subjects about which the people are to pray. A time of silence is given following each directed prayer thought.

Intercessory prayer methods might be accomplished by each worshiper writing on a provided card a certain concern, or person for which they would like prayer. These requests are received in a tray; then the tray is taken to another section of the sanctuary, where persons take out cards. After all cards are distributed, a period of silence is provided during which each worshiper lifts up intercessory prayers for the concern and person named on his card.

Again, worshipers may write a concern for which they want a specific person to pray. The person's name whom they request to pray for the concern is also placed at the bottom of the card. Cards are collected. Then the church secretary mails them to the persons requested. Throughout the week the request is prayed about.

One of the better ways of involving a congregation in prayer is by *responsive litanies, dialogue,* or *unison* prayers.

Creative silent periods in public worship afford opportunities for meditation and prayer. They need to be provided often.

Each worshiper may be given a flower as he enters the sanctuary. During the prayer time he is asked to contemplate its beauty, symmetry, and uniqueness. Then, "Thank God for what the flower says to you about Him."

Worshipers may be asked to focus their thoughts or eyes on

their hands, or feet, etc. While the leader talks about the hand, for example, the burdens it has carried, the good or evil it has done, the mystery of it—the worshiper prays whatever he feels of thankfulness, confession, petition, intercession.

Flashbacks are bringing back to mind the situations, persons, happenings of the past week which had special significance to the worshiper. The leader of worship invites the worshipers to recall these occasions, and then to pray what is appropriate and needed, according to God's will.

Creatively Convey and Dramatize Scripture The object of Scripture reading is to communicate the message. There is an abundance of translations of the Bible in living language that are understandable, and most usable in worship. Likewise, portions of the Scriptures have been paraphrased creatively in a way that conveys the core meaning. Have worshipers paraphrase the Scripture lesson in their own words. Give them a few minutes to do so. Several might share their work with the congregation; or, as the Scriptures are read each worshiper may express his feelings about the lesson in various gestures.

One most impressive method of Scripture reading (if the passage lends itself to it) is for the leader to sing or chant each line, making up his own melody. Then the congregation repeats each line and melody after the leader. With practice, this rhythmic antiphonal participation can be meaningful and beautiful, especially to children and youth.

Interpretive pantomiming of the Scripture reading may be done simultaneously with the reading. This requires persons trained in the art, whose gestures are sensitive and tastefully done. When appropriately done, the feeling of the Scriptures comes alive. Such should not be done to entertain the worshipers, but to convey the interior reality.

A group may be selected to act out the Scriptures; or, as a narrator reads the passages, one person from the congregation may pantomime in dramatic form the actions or scenes described.

In some youth-directed services, Scriptures have been written

on the back of paper plates or on paper airplanes. Then at the
indicated point in the service, the plates or planes are thrown
into the congregation from the balcony. Those who catch a plate,
stand up and read the Scripture verses. Similarly, Scriptures
printed on small strips of paper have been inserted into balloons
as they are blown up. Then at the time indicated, the balloons
are released. Those catching them read the Scriptures aloud to
the worshipers.

Convert the Deductive Sermon Traditionally, the worshiper
has been a passive listener. The clergyman proclaimed the
Word; the worshiper looked to him as an authority figure, as
the best educated in the community, hence the chief source of
information and inspiration. Consequently the pulpiteer assumed
a didactic, deductive, dogmatic stance in preaching. The congregation was told the conclusion by the so-called authority. Logic,
reason, debate, proof approaches were utilized.

Passivity for the worshiper is no longer valid today. The
worshiper's level of education often surpasses the minister's.
Communication and growth is accomplished through interchange
of thought and dialogical involvement. Because of this, the style
of the sermon and presentation is greatly affected.

In contemporary worship, monological preaching needs to be
inductive, attempting to involve the listener in thinking and
feeling. The presentation method is conversational in tone, non-
defensive and open in approach. It does not *preach at* the
worshipers, but *thinks with* them, taking them on a journey,
looking at various scenes, until they see the conclusion or
destination themselves.

The minister uses many rhetorical questions and human
interest events to involve the worshiper's thoughts and emotions.
Thus, the worshiper participates in the sermon. Instead of
beginning in the ancient world with the Scripture setting or
lesson, the minister begins the sermon with a human interest
experience, problem, or question. He surveys this with the
congregation, looking at it from all sides, focusing interest. He

does not answer or assume a conclusion; rather, he reaches back to the Word for light to illumine thought and conscience. He points to the gospel, and brings to bear the resources of the Christian faith on the contemporary issue. He pays attention to feelings, movements, psychological methods. The minister does not identify with the final answer too early. He assumes the congregation has some intelligence and can think through to conclusions. He seeks to create an openness which allows questions and diverse views. He allows the Word to be heard in the most creative, self-authenticating ways possible. He has a disarming, honest, warm, conversational approach in contrast to the loud, dogmatic, cocksure, bombastic, oratorical method. The contemporary style is not to talk *down to* or *preach a proposition at* worshipers. It is to walk with them, to share views, and to feel experiences that lead to Christ. It is not an easy assignment but a most rewarding challenge. The day of preaching is not over. The gospel must still be proclaimed. The way it is carried, however, needs updating.

Various other methods of communicating the Word involve the worshiper, such as the dialogue, the talk-back, role-playing, discussion, parable, interview, open-ended films, drama, and multimedia presentations.

Brighten the Atmosphere with Color Until recent years vestments have been confined to pulpit, lectern, and altar table. A great deal of contemporary atmosphere, however, can be created with the use of banners. They should be changed frequently in color, size, and shape as well as composition. Burlap, silk, felt, print cloth in stripes or plaids, vinyl, drapery material, corduroy, upholstery, see-through mesh, and aluminum foil are materials that can be utilized with a bit of imagination. They should be designed by someone experienced in textiles.

Banners may reinforce a seasonal emphasis of the church calendar, or focus upon a sermon theme or Christian doctrine; complement a festival celebration, or reflect a contemporary social concern. Banners may contain verbal texts, symbols, pictures, or recognizable objects that can be identified by their shape. The message must be terse, provocative, and significant. Each of the major celebration days is wrought with unlimited possibilities for banners.

Banners may be carried in the processional and placed in a flag stand on the chancel area, or the banners may be hung by a swivel hook at various places around the sanctuary nave, chancel, or in the foyer.

This, like all other innovations, needs to be kept in balance. Do not go to seed on banners. Knowing when to stop is a virtue of the wise and sensitive!

Hanging long strips of brightly colored cloth or crepe paper adds gaiety to what may otherwise be a drab, dark room. Each worshiper may also be given a crepe stole in varied colors to drape around his neck.

Choir robes can be purchased in a variety of psychedelic colors, plus the addition of varied stoles that may emphasize the liturgical seasons.

To many pastors, the black pulpit robe is too mournful. Why should not the pastor have a varied number of colorful robes and stoles? or, if not a robe, why must he be confined to a dark suit? Some ministers are experimenting with colorful ponchos, with large symbols sewed on them. Others favor more of a form-fitting cassock.

One church has a series of lights whereby the dossal curtain of the chancel can be changed to all the liturgical colors. It creates a meaningful variety of moods for worship.

Balloons can be utilized. If filled with helium they can be tied on ten-foot lengths of string and scores of them tacked to the back of the pews, creating a substitute ceiling of color, or, in some cases balloons (if not filled with helium gas) may be dropped over the congregation from the balcony—then tossed up by those upon whom they fall.

Dress up the Bulletin There have come across my desk all kinds of contemporary church bulletins. These have been given to worshipers as they arrive for services and contain the order and content of the worship. With slogans, line cartoons, and creative arrangements, the spirit of celebration and joy can be conveyed.

Many churches have on their Sunday bulletin a picture of their church facility with address and other routine information. Strange, since all of the people present, members and visitors alike, know the church by location and design or they wouldn't be there! Such a bulletin conveys the view that the church building is of supreme importance, and that brick and mortar compose the church.

How much more important it is to have bulletins that convey something suggesting Christian truth—such as Christian symbols, Biblical scenes, etchings, or nature scenes. One bulletin I received had on the outside, CHOOSE LIFE, in large letters; then on the inside were the sections: TEACH US OF LIFE; TELL US OF LIFE; TRIGGER US FOR LIFE with appropriate line drawings. Creative young people had their hand in it.

Some churches week after week list their church leaders on the back of the bulletin. One gets bored seeing the names. Furthermore, those whose names appear become more concerned about being "seen of men," than the "serving of men." If you do not believe this to be so, wait until a name is accidentally omitted or misspelled!

Could this not be utilized for the listing of penetrating thoughts, opportunities for service, or information about the Christian enterprise?

Contemporize the Environment   You say you're stuck with what you have? You inherited what people a generation ago planned? That may be true—yet it is no excuse to do nothing.

Look at the outside—where worshipers approach the sanctuary. Is there any place for a banner, posters, lawn signs, streamers? Is there any place to tie balloons? This affords some opportunity.

The narthex or vestibule is a useful resource for displaying banners, art, and friendliness that set the tone of the church.

It is the sanctuary, however, that has been most inflexible. The traditional architecture design separated clergy and people, giving the impression that worship is a professional performance by the clergyman. Churches with flexible spaces can enhance a festive mood merely by creatively arranging the chairs. One church changes the pews each week. Another has placed the pews in a square around the communion table in the center. This creates an intimacy that preserves family. Though the furniture may be attached as is the case in most sanctuaries, there are many things that can be done to create a more festive, contemporary feel.

Take a look at your sanctuary. Does it emanate depression or uplift? Is there icy austerity or a mellow friendliness? Is the atmosphere one of rigidity or joy? Is there any way the minister and choir can be made closer to the worshipers?

Some churches have made a mobile pulpit and altar table. The Perkins Chapel at Southern Methodist University has derived a mobile, transparent curtain completely closing off the chancel, upon which a wide variety of images and colors can be simultaneously projected. The screen can be removed in minutes.

The walls afford the opportunity to place creative symbols, banners, posters, and slogans for freshness and variety. The electronic media make possible all kinds of different scenery and figures suggesting celebration. There are many things that can be accomplished also with candles, colored burlap, sculpture, and incense.

A Warning   It is hoped that these few suggestions will stimulate other creative, fresh experiments in worship. A warning, however, is in order: In my opinion, it is quite easy to become too mod and foolishly innovative. One can look upon worship as programmish—as a performance for people to enjoy. Worship is an offering to God. It is *He* we strive to please. Unconsciously, the planner may be motivated to manipulate people, using all kinds of dramatic and psychological tricks. We may seek dramatic or emotional materials and techniques to move people—hence, worship becomes too subjective, too man-directed. It can become a disjointed hodge-podge of dull, unfamiliar symbols, unrelated to the past, without theological support and purely mechanical.

All efforts must be utilized to make worship meaningful, in good taste, orderly and acceptable unto God who is our spiritual worship. Keeping theological integrity is basic to whatever worship forms are assumed.

Section 2

CELEBRATIVE
ENCOUNTERS

Section 2

CELEBRATIVE ENCOUNTERS

A CELEBRATION OF LOVE

Music for Gathering (*recorded or live*) "What the World Needs Now Is Love, Sweet Love" and "They'll Know We Are Christians by Our Love"

Opening Sentences

LEADER   Dear friends! Let us love one another, for love comes from God.

PEOPLE   We love because God first loved us.

LEADER   If someone says, "I love God," yet hates his brother, he is a liar.

PEOPLE   For he cannot love God, whom he has not seen, if he does not love his brother, whom he has seen.

LEADER   This, then, is the command that Christ gave us: He who loves God must love his brother also.

PEOPLE   O Divine Master, grant that we may not so much seek to be consoled as to console; to be understood as to understand; to be loved as to love. Amen.

SONG   "People of Peace, Children of Love" (*three verses*)

BRIDGE   (*after third refrain*)

Prayer of Confession (*congregation seated*)   Eternal God, we pray that Your mercy will be upon us as we confess to You our failures in love and friendship. We have talked about brotherhood and have shown indifference, anger, and hostility. We have talked about love and have calculated the times we have forgiven. We have talked about service and have selfishly thrust others aside that we might advance our own ambitions. We have talked about bearing our own burdens and have viciously blamed others in order to cover our own shortcomings. We have talked about sacrifice and have rested in comfort while others were weighed down by oppression, injustice, and sorrow. Forgive our neglected vows, our broken promises, the sins we confess, and those we dare not name. And in the name of Him who was crucified for sin, grant Your forgiveness to us. Amen.

Silent Confession   Lord is it I? Lord, is it I? O Christ, how far was I from You at any time when love and faithfulness by me were so profaned; when another's trust in me was sold for gain; and love and hope and longing left bleeding to their thorns?

Declaration of Pardon

LEADER   This is how God showed His love for us: He sent His only Son into the world that we might have life through Him. This is what love is: It is not that we have loved God, but that He loved us and sent His Son to be the means by which our sins are forgiven.

Scripture Reading 1 Corinthians 13 (*paraphrased*)   Though you speak with tongues of men and of angels and have not human understanding, you are a noisy gong or a clanging cymbal. And though you can explain the Scriptures in learned fashion and quote from the latest commentaries with complete assurance, even if you master the art of holding twelve-year-old boys spellbound as you expound the Minor Prophets, and still have not human understanding, you are nothing. If you put every penny (and dollar, too) into the offering plate each Sunday morning, if you work in the church kitchen every time there is a supper, if you learn to call all members of your congregation by their first names, yea, even if you come into the House of God each time its doors are opened, and have not human understanding, you gain nothing.

Understanding is patient, kind, not jealous of another's good fortune, not self-exalting, or rude. Understanding does not insist on its own way, is not irritable, or resentful. It is touched by sadness when someone else has unhappiness, and finds great delight in another's good fortune. Human understanding is being able to take whatever happens, always believing the best of people. Human understanding never, never gives up in reaching out with compassion.[1]

"Now" Reading   "Make Love, Not War"

> "All you need is love."
> That's the way the Beatles say IT.
> "Make love, not war."
> That's the way the peace marchers say IT.
> "Love is the answer."
> This is another way to say IT.
> But what is "IT"? What is being said?
> What is LOVE?
> Is it just a nice friendly feeling?
> Is it guaranteed
>   by growing a beard and carrying a placard?
>   or by going to church, singing the right
>   hymns, saying the right words, giving the
>   right amount of money?
> The kind of love which is a healing answer
>   to a very infirm (there is the possibility
>   that the sickness is terminal) world is no
>   simple, easy answer.
> It is a simple matter to make the affirmation
>   that "love is the answer."
> But it is not a simple matter to bring that
>   affirmation to life, where confirmation of
>   it requires sweat and tears
>   and perhaps blood.

Talking is one thing—it's cheap.
Doing is another—and it costs!
Love is not an idea. LOVE can't really be *said*.
 LOVE must be *done*.
Love means relationship, personal involvement,
 honest sharing at the deepest levels.
Therefore . . . do not be a lover who
 "talks a good game."
You are not called to talk about Love.
You are called to LOVE.[2]

SONG   "Love Is The Answer"

Prayer (*by all*)   O Father, Creator of all sorts and conditions of men, make us realize that we are one creation of Your love: have-nots and haves, unlovely and lovely, the graceless and the dignified, the foolish and the wise, we are all Your family, inheritors of Your bounty. Enliven us, O God, to claim our every family relationship through You, to trace our kinship with every man or woman, to love every brother.

Redeem us more and more, Lord, from aloofness. Forbid that we should withhold from anyone anything we can spare. Spare us from using any person or group, from handing on old caricatures or fondling imagined superiorities. For we deeply know that our common bonds with all persons open us up to You, while our small differences and enmities split us off, narrow us, dry us up.

In Christ's love, keep us from attributing to others the failings we hate in ourselves: laziness, vanity, arrogance, doubledealing. Rather, enable us to search out in our neighbor what we honor and covet for our own life: strength, humor, kindness, humility, skill, endurance. Show us, O God, that we need one another, hold one another up when faltering, enlarge one another's spirits. . . . we pray for warmth to open up cliques into wide fellowship, clannishness into wide community, small sympathies and narrow goals into the new wholeness of human understanding. We pray in the name of our Lord, the Christ. Amen.

Sermon   (*based on the song* "They'll Know We Are Christians by Our Love." [3] *One verse and chorus to be sung by* CONGREGATION *and* CHOIR *between each meditation.*)

VERSE 1

> We are one in the Spirit, etc.

MEDITATION 1   They Will Know We Are Christians by OUR LOVING ATTITUDES.

VERSE 2

> We will walk with each other, etc.

MEDITATION 2   They Will Know We Are Christians by OUR LOVING RELATIONSHIPS.

VERSE 3

> We will work with each other, etc.

MEDITATION 3   They Will Know We Are Christians by OUR LOVING DEEDS.

VERSE 4

> All praise to the Father, etc.

Dismissal   (*turning to the person on your left*) _____ (*first name, if possible*), as God loves us, so I love you.

Departure Music   "What The World Needs Now Is Love, Sweet Love"

CELEBRATE! LOVE! LIVE!

CONGREGATION *gathers and is seated in two rows of chairs facing each other.*

LEADER We are here to celebrate: Let's celebrate! Now is the time to live, to come to the Father who creates us, to sing to the Lord who frees us, to dance with the Spirit who fills us.

PEOPLE Yes, now is the time to celebrate.

LEADER Let us invite the whole world to join us in praising God.

PEOPLE Let us invite our leaders to glorify His name.

LEADER Let us invite the happy people and the sad people to speak with us today.

PEOPLE We ask all people living and alone, the blacks and the whites who have no rights, the unemployed and the angry poor, the haves and the have-nots, to tell the truth in love.

LEADER Let us invite those who love us to eat and drink with us.

PEOPLE We invite our friends to know our joy, to those we love to know our Lord, and those we long to have beside us now to celebrate with us.

A PARAPHRASE OF 1 CORINTHIANS 13

If I can sing "Green Grow the Rushes Ho" from memory or preach like Billy Graham, but say nothing loving, I am nothing but an untuned electric guitar or a set of drums. If I have ESP and am learned as Einstein, or can blow up Camp Montgomery by the exertion of faith alone, but have no love in my heart, I am as empty as outer space. If I put my whole wardrobe in the Goodwill Box, or set myself afire like a Buddhist monk, but do them without love, I accomplish exactly zero.

Love does not lose its cool. It is thoughtful of others' feelings. Love is not a green-eyed monster. Love is not snobbish and forms no cliques. It is not rude, crude and unattractive. It does not insist on its own way like Lucy does in Peanuts. Love is not like parents before they've had their morning coffee. Love does not feel the same way I do when a teacher asks a question on the final that has never been discussed in class. Love does not spread gossip but instead is glad to have it squashed. Love trusts in the strength and righteousness of God. It sees the doughnut and not the hole. Love puts up with small irritations constantly.

Love is for keeps. As for Ouija boards and political speeches and Ph.D.'s, they will croak. Our data is incomplete, and tea leaves sometimes lie. But when love reigns, war and hunger and strife will end. When I was a kid I talked baby talk, my thoughts were immature, my reasoning for the birds. But when I grew up, I began to mature. As long as we are trapped inside these human bodies, we can only partially understand the wonders of the universe, but one day God's knowledge will be ours, and we will know Him as completely as He knows us. So faith, hope and love will last forever, but I'll put my money on love.[4]

HYMN   "Rejoice Ye Pure In Heart" (*first verse*)

LEADER   We are here to love and to learn to love! Let's love!

FIRST READER   You have heard that it used to be said, "An eye for an eye and a tooth for a tooth," but I tell you, don't resist the man who wants to do you harm. If a man hits your right cheek, turn the other to him as well.

SECOND READER   Love is a RISKY business!

FIRST READER   If you love only those who love you, what credit is that to you? And if you exchange greetings with your own circle, are you doing anything exceptional?

SECOND READER   Love IS a risky business.

FIRST READER   To love is to be available—to be involved up to the hilt. Real love is not concerned about limitations but only about opportunities.

SECOND READER   LOVE is a risky business.

FIRST READER   Love does not carefully calculate the cost; it does not keep a ledger of profit and loss, for the left hand does not know what the right hand is doing. Love is a spendthrift. It does not measure itself out with an eyedropper. Love is extravagant. Love seeks out a need and never stops giving.

BOTH READERS   Love is a risky business, for it costs—it costs EVERYTHING!

SONG   "They'll Know We Are Christians by Our Love"

LEADER   We are here to live and to learn to live in Christ.

Words of Life (*spoken by various persons in group*)

FIRST PERSON "For in him we live and move and have our being" (Acts 17:28).

SECOND PERSON "God sent his only Son into the world, so that we might live through him" (1 John 4:9).

THIRD PERSON "I am come that they might have life, and have it abundantly" (John 10:10).

FOURTH PERSON "For me to live is Christ, and to die is gain" (Philippians 1:21).

FIFTH PERSON "I have been crucified with Christ; it is no longer I who live, but Christ who lives in me" (Galatians 2:20).

SIXTH PERSON "If possible, live peaceably with all" (Romans 12:18).

SEVENTH PERSON "If we live by the Spirit, let us also walk by the Spirit" (Galatians 5:25).

HYMN "Take My Life and Let It Be" (*verses 1 and 5*)

LEADER Shalom!

PEOPLE Shalom!

CELEBRATION OF JOY [5]

Salutation

LEADER Praise the Lord.

PEOPLE O what a beautiful day.

LEADER Let's sing, dance, and express ourselves in celebration.

PEOPLE In celebrating to the Lord our God.

SONG "Zip-A-De-Doo-Dah"

Confession of Sin

LEADER Have mercy on me, O God, according to Thy steadfast love;

PEOPLE   According to Thy abundant mercy blot out my transgressions.

LEADER   Wash me thoroughly from my iniquity,

PEOPLE   And cleanse me from my sin!

LEADER   In Thee, O Lord, do I take refuge; let me never be put to shame!

PEOPLE   In Thy righteousness deliver me and rescue me; incline Thy ear to me, and save me!

LEADER   For Thou art my rock and my fortress.

PEOPLE   Rescue me, O my God, from the hand of the wicked, For Thou, O Lord, art my hope.

Prayers of Intercession   (*Have persons write concerns on a card. Collect cards, then redistribute. Persons pray silently for the concern indicated on the card received.*)

The Old Testament Lesson

LEADER   Hear the Word of God from the Old Testament, as it is written in Psalm 150. (*Other Scriptures may be substituted.*)

PEOPLE   Thanks be to Thee, O God.

Community Witness   (*Persons from congregation give one sentence testimonies suggested by Scripture reading.*)

The New Testament Lesson

LEADER   Hear the Word of God from the New Testament, as it is written in Matthew 25:14–31. (*Or substitute other Scripture.*)

PEOPLE   Praise be to Thee, O God.

Community Witness   (*Persons from congregation give one sentence testimonies suggested by Scripture reading.*)

The Sharing of the Good News

THE GIVING (*all the people*)   You give but little when you give of your possessions. It is when you give of yourself that you truly give.

SONG   "Sons of God"

The Great Thanksgiving O Lord, our Father, please accept our offering of praise and thanksgiving for life in Jesus Christ. Here and now we pray for cleansing and renewal of spirit. We dedicate ourselves to You, through Jesus Christ our Lord. Amen.

The Meal *The experiencing of bread:* "As they were eating, Jesus took a small loaf of bread and blessed it and broke it apart and gave it to the disciples and said, 'Take it and eat it, for this is my body'" (Matthew 26:26, 27, LB).

The experiencing of drinking: "And he took a cup of wine and gave thanks for it and gave it to them and said, 'Each one drink from it, for this is my blood, sealing the New Covenant. It is poured out to forgive the sins of multitudes'" (Matthew 26:27–29, LB).

The experiencing of togetherness: "Now you are no longer strangers to God and foreigners to heaven, but you are members of God's very own family, citizens of God's country, and you belong in God's household with every other Christian" (Ephesians 2:19, LB).

The Benediction Go in peace. You are forgiven. Jesus Christ Himself has reconciled the past.

SONG OF RESURRECTION "When the Saints Go Marching In"

CELEBRATE LIFE! [6]

Prelude "Paintings at an Exhibition"—Moussorgsky *During the prelude listen to the music. Let it carry you along and remind you of experiences in your life. It is a different kind of music but life is different every day. The music is loud and soft, fast*

*and slow, new and different, just as life is. Let yourself become
a part of the music and a part of the service.*

Call to Worship Psalm 98 (NEB)

UNISON INVOCATION Lord, I do have this life! I do want to
live it to the full. Don't let me miss anything good, nor scorn
those who find what I have missed. Lord, give me freedom,
freedom to rejoice in Your gifts of life and love. Lord, give
me faith, faith to be happy and to praise You with all my
strength. Enable me this day to worship in spirit and in truth.
Keep my thoughts from wandering. Cause me to heed how I
hear Your Word. Give me understanding that I may receive
the message You send. Open my mind and heart that I may
communicate and respond to those who seek communication.
Amen.

Invitation to Worship   LET'S CELEBRATE!

LEADER

> Now is the time to live;
> to come to the Father who creates us,
> to sing to the Lord who frees us,
> to dance with the Spirit who fills us.

CONGREGATION   Yes, now is the time to celebrate!

LEADER Let us invite the whole world to join us in praising
God.

CONGREGATION We invite the sky to thunder His Word, the
earth to rumble in praise, the sea to swirl with song.

LEADER Let us invite the whole city to worship with us.

CONGREGATION We call the traffic in the streets, department
stores, revolving doors, elevators, and all the people in the
yellow pages to stop and shout His Name.

LEADER Let us invite our leaders to glorify His Name.

CONGREGATION We summon doctor, president, movie star, pro-
fessor, clown, to step down and kneel with us.

LEADER Let us invite the happy people and the sad people
to speak with us today.

CONGREGATION We ask all people living alone, the blacks and the whites who have no rights, the unemployed and the angry poor, the haves and the have-nots, to tell the truth in love.

LEADER Let us extend an open invitation to one and all to join in one full circle of joy.

CONGREGATION Join the circle, Lord, and make our joy complete.

SONG "Mighty Clouds of Joy"

Confession and Absolution (*to be spoken by the congregation to each other*)

LEADER Let us be honest with God and with each other and confess our sins in order that we might receive the great forgiveness of God through Jesus Christ:

(*Both sides of the congregation turn to center aisle and face each other.* LEFT SIDE *of congregation speaks confession;* RIGHT SIDE *responds.*)

LEFT SIDE Lord, our God, we sure have a way of messing up our lives. We often doubt You, we often ignore You, we often insult You, but we still call You Father.

We are weak, we are human but we are baptized.

We hear Your Word, we have Your world,

We bear Your image, and we are Yours.

We are brothers together in Christ Jesus, who come to You now to ask for power and forgiveness in His Name.

RIGHT SIDE In the Name of Jesus Christ, I speak His Word to you: I am one of you, I died and rose as one of you, I know who you are, I feel what you feel.

I forgive your wrongs, and so I give you power to change your lives and to see your worth as sons of God with Me.

(RIGHT SIDE *of congregation speaks confession;* LEFT SIDE *responds.*)

RIGHT SIDE Lord, our God, we sure have a way of messing up our lives. We often doubt You, we often ignore You, we often insult You, but we still call You Father.

We are weak, we are human but we are baptized.

We hear Your Word, we have Your world,

We bear Your image, and we are Yours.

We are brothers together in Christ Jesus, who come to You now to ask for power and forgiveness in His Name.

LEFT SIDE In the Name of Jesus Christ, I speak His Word to you: I am one of you, I died and rose as one of you, I know who you are, I feel what you feel.

I forgive your wrongs, and so I give you power to change your lives and to see your worth as sons of God with Me.

ALL Thank You, Lord, for giving us new life! That's real life, and that's living! Amen.

SONG "The Spirit of the Lord Is Upon Us"

Unison Prayer for Offering (*standing*) Almighty Father, bless and keep each one of us this day. Let this offering be used to communicate our love and concern to others in this world. Help us to spread this celebration of life to all so that peace may come on earth again. Bless these gifts and the giver. In Jesus' Name. Amen.

Meditation A teen-age girl reached out in reconciliation to her parents last summer. There had been considerable turmoil in the family, and difficulty of communication between the girl and her parents. She went off to camp and later wrote a letter which said in part:

Dear Mom and Dad: I just want to say a few things to you. I mean it's so much easier to say it in a letter than to your face. I want to say how great you guys have been to me and how ungrateful I've been to you. I want to tell you that I really think you guys are great and I love you very much. See, now I couldn't say that to your face. I get embarrassed to say "I love you" to my own parents. I'm really sorry if you've been disappointed in me but I think I'm learning. I'm glad you guys are my parents. I love and miss you very much."

I wonder if young people have any idea how much a mother and father yearn and wait for such a letter and what it means—those little signs of love. Why is it so hard for us to say to those we're closest to: "I love you; I think you're great. You're beautiful. I admire you."

When we can bring ourselves to do this, it's like the sun turns on. It's like flowers starting to bloom.

Is there someone to whom you might reach out in reconciliation and hope today with a letter, a phone call, a hug, or a squeeze of the hand? You can be an agent of reconciliation.

Jesus put His body on the line to reach out to all of us. He is there in the bread and wine, saying to us: "I'm your brother, and I love you. Come and eat and drink with Me, and let's be friends." [7] (Reprinted from the February, 1971, issue of *Pulpit Digest*.)

SONG   "Bridge Over Troubled Waters"

Dismissal

> The peace of God go with us all
> Wherever life may lead.
> The love we've shared go with us, too,
> For strength in time of need.
>
> The love of God go with us now
> At home, or work, or play.
> And permeate our daily lives
> In all we do and say. Amen.[8]

CELEBRATION OF GATHERING

This service is for an informal conference or retreat setting. For a more formal setting, eliminate the first part.

The Act of Gathering (*For an informal setting, in an open area, with not too large a group. An appropriate gathering might* *be a conference, retreat, or meeting of persons who are strangers or casual acquaintainces. When the people have arrived at the designated location, the* LEADER *asks all to hold hands in a large circle. Then he begins "the snail," moving the line single file while holding hands, into a smaller circle—smaller, smaller and smaller—until the group finally is in a compact, compressed gathering. This will be great fun, a good ice-breaker, hilarious with laughter if done properly. When the group is tightly knit, the* LEADER *in the center says,* "We are celebrating our gathering! Take a minute right where you are to greet those at your side—giving name, address, hobby, favorite food." *After the greeting, the* LEADER *will say,* "Let us sing as we take a seat around the worship center.")

SONG   "In His Name" (*with guitar player leading*)

Sentences of Gathering (*either in silence or led by* LITURGIST)
I've searched for community in many places, Jesus. I was often looking in the wrong places. Now, in this moment, which many people would label "loneliness" or "nothingness," I want to thank You, Jesus. In this moment—in this place with these other persons—I have found community where and as it is. It seems to me it is Your gift. I am here with these others for a short time. Soon, I will be gone, but I won't be searching so desperately anymore. I know I must accept community where You offer it to me. I accept it in this moment. Thank You, Jesus.[9]

Summons

LITURGIST   We have come to this place as individuals, from different backgrounds, each with various goals, interests and abilities, yet we gather in community.

PEOPLE   We are called to be the church in the world. We are not a building, but a vibrating, pulsating people, set in history. We are not the spectators, but the participants in this life which God gave us.

LITURGIST   We remember that Jesus said, "Where two or three are gathered in My Name, I am in the midst of them."

PEOPLE   We affirm Christ's Lordship. He affirms our total life.

We celebrate this because we are His church. We celebrate together because, being many, we are one.

LITURGIST One of our contemporaries, Dietrich Bonhoeffer, has said, "Only in this world is Christ, Christ." It is in this world that we must live.

PEOPLE We worship to perceive and to act out again what it means to live as Christians in this age. For the sake of this transforming life, we praise and celebrate our God. Amen.

SONG "Hey, Hey, Anybody Listenin'?"

The Act of Praise (*in unison*)

Alive!
We thank Thee
O Lord whose finger touched our dust,
O Lord who gave us breath.

We thank Thee, Lord, who gave us sight and sense
  to see the flowers,
  to hear the wind,
  to feel the waters in our hand,

  to sleep with the night and wake with the sun,
  to stand upon this star,
  to sing Thy praise,
  to hear Thy voice.

Our hearts are stirred with each new sight and sound—

Like a stream, the whole world pours into our lives, our
  eyes, our hands, and fills our souls with living gladness.
O Lord, our God,
How excellent is Thy name.
Amen!

SONG "What Has Drawn Us Together"

The Act of Evaluation

LEADER We have been given life, yet we have difficulty in knowing ourselves. Even when by human standards we are most humble, measured by the life of the Master, we lack humility. It is difficult to make a self-evaluation. Therefore, let us bow before the One who has made us and see our lives in the light of His presence.

LEADER AND PEOPLE

God, our Father!
Make us discontent with things the way they are in the world and in our lives.
Teach us to blush again for:
  our tawdry deals;
  the arrogant but courteous prejudice;
  our willing use of the rights and privileges other men are unfairly denied.

Make us notice the stains when people get spilled on. Jar our complacency; expose our excuses; get us involved in the life of this church, this city, this world, and help us to find integrity once again that we may in some way keep within reach of the Jesus whom we claim to follow. Amen!

Confession   (*private, to be read and thought about silently*)

I am tired of being
hard,
      tight,
            controlled
tensed against the invasion of novelty,
armed against tenderness,
      afraid of softness,
I am tired of
directing my world,
making,
      doing,
            shaping.

(*public*)
LITURGIST   Let us admit our insensitivity.
PEOPLE   Lord, forgive us for not sensing.
LITURGIST   Let us admit our self-centeredness.

PEOPLE   Lord, forgive us for not sensing.

LITURGIST   Let us admit our smallness of spirit.

PEOPLE   Lord, forgive us for not sensing.

LITURGIST   Let us admit our tendency to condemn.

PEOPLE   Lord, forgive us for not sensing.

LITURGIST   Let us admit our fickle loyalty.

PEOPLE   Lord, forgive us for not sensing.

LITURGIST   Let us admit our prejudices.

PEOPLE   Lord, forgive us for not sensing.

LITURGIST   Let us admit we are a part of the problem.

PEOPLE   Lord, forgive us for not sensing.

Word of Possibility   The Lord God says: Crawl out of those tombs and prisons—there is a world of light and freedom waiting. The higher and more secure we build the barricades of care and caution to protect ourselves, the deeper grows the grave we call life. Have faith in the Giver of life and let life be free! The Word is Life. Say *yes* to the Word of Life. Let us rise up and praise His holy Name.

Declaration of Release   Free at last! Free at last! Thank God Almighty, we're free at last! Amen.

Hearing the Word

SCRIPTURE   Ephesians 4:1–7, 11–16

NEW TESTIMONY   "We're Enemies, God"

What's wrong with me, God?

I hurt my friends
and say rotten things about them.
I brag to them
and use them all like little steps
to make myself feel taller.
I pretend to be concerned
about the things they say,
but what I really want to do
is to enjoy their company
like friendly pets who do not bite.

If I stop and think
about the things I do
I get mad at myself
for being selfish
and stupid and thoughtless.
But tomorrow
I'll probably go out
and do the same things again
without realizing what I do.

Why can't I change?
I know what's wrong
but that doesn't solve anything.

Maybe—
Yes, maybe the problem
is something much deeper.
Maybe the things I do
are just the surface sores,
sores that I can scratch
to avoid looking deeper.
Maybe there's some
deep internal bleeding
that is making me so frantic.

Maybe the real sickness
is a kind of wound inside
that comes from trying
to tear away from God
and live without him.

Maybe God is the trouble after all,
and he won't stop the pain
till I give in to him.
For he keeps giving me hell inside
till I surrender all my pride.

Well, if that is true,
I hate you, God.
I hate anyone who hurts me,
exposes me,
or makes me look weak.

I hate you
because you can see through me
and find me
no matter where I run,
because you can break my brain
like a bad dream.

Why don't you leave me alone, God?
Why do you hunt me
as if I were a wanted man?
What do you want with me?
Do you enjoy torturing me?

I'm just a man.
Am I so important?
We're enemies, God.
How can you change that?
How?

If only there were someone
who could stand between us
with a hand on my shoulder
and a hand on yours
to mediate our differences.

Or is that the role
that Jesus Christ, the Jew,
has been waiting centuries
to play for me
and you? [10]

Words of the Community Homily by the LEADER, "Community in Christ"
SONG "The Man From Galilee"

The Act of Doing
MEDITATION "What in the World Are You Doing"

Christians talk
    and talk and talk
Piling word upon word
World without end.

Principles and policies
Theories and politics
Theologies and
    abstractions . . .
It is better to speak one
    word with clarity
    by demonstration,
    in the idiom of action,
Than to speak
    ten thousand words
    in the unknown tongue
    of much speaking
    and no doing.[11]

THE COLLECTION   This is not a collection of monies, but a lifting of our whole life and work before God. The money given by you is but a symbolic offering of your energies and vitality, as well as your weakness before God.

Community Prayers   (*spontaneous prayers for the concerns of the community of faith*)

The Act of Going Out

LEADER   We have gathered here again—
We have heard the Word again.

PEOPLE   And what is required in response to this Word?

LEADER   The Lord has told us:
                    Do justice—
                    love mercy and kindness—
                    walk humble in His presence.

PEOPLE   So we have been told before—so we have heard it again, and yet we remain so much a part of the problem.

LEADER   Yes, we are part of the problem. If we go forth into the world and respond to His love in all that we do, we can become part of the answer.

PEOPLE   May we go forth to become part of the answer.

CELEBRATING COMMUNITY

Preparation Explanation We have searched for community in many places. We often have looked in the wrong locations, looking futilely and hopelessly for belonging, acceptance, fellowship. In the presence of Jesus' friends, we are offered community. It is ours for the acceptance. Let us realize community in Christ as we worship.

Gathering Music (*guitars*)
"What Has Drawn Us Together?"
"I Come Tired"
"In His Name"

Summons
LITURGIST We have come to this place as individuals, each with varied backgrounds, abilities, interests, and goals, yet we gather to celebrate community.
PEOPLE We are called to be the church in the world. We are not a building; we are people. We are not spectators; we are participants in this life which God gave us.
LITURGIST Jesus said, "Where two or three are gathered in my name, there am I in their midst."
PEOPLE Together we celebrate God, because being many, in Christ we are one.
UNISON We praise and celebrate our God. As we worship, we act out again what it means to live as Christians in this age.
SONG "They'll Know We Are Christians by Our Love"
THE WORD FROM AN ANCIENT LETTER Ephesians 2:14–21

The Barriers Dividing Us

LEADER   Each worshiper was given a paper bag when entering.
You are now to put it over your head. It is a barrier between
you and your neighbors.

PRAYER OF CONFESSION (*by* LEADER)   We have many barriers
that separate us from one another, symbolized by these bags
over our heads. Let us admit to ourselves and to God that we
are self-centered in many ways. We couldn't care less about
others. (*Silence*) Let us admit to ourselves and God our smallness of spirit that doesn't see beyond our own walls. (*Silence*)
Let us admit the barriers of prejudice, hatred, exclusiveness
and superiority that we build between ourselves and others.
(*Silence*) Let us admit our tendency to condemn and our two-
faced disloyalty that shuts others out. (*Silence*) Let us admit
our mistrust of others that keeps them at arm's length and de-
stroys relationships. (*Silence*)

Lord, we are where our sins have placed us—in the dark!
separated! alienated! Not until we repent, and become brothers
and sisters to others, and open with You, and intend to lead a
new life and be more loving, can we take the bag off. Lord,
forgive us and help us to be able to remove the barriers pre-
venting community in Christ's Spirit. Amen.

Lifting the Veil   (*If out-of-doors, or in a setting where it is possible, the bags can now be taken off, collected and burned—symbolizing destroying of the walls dividing people and burning the
sins away.*)

LEADER (*as bags are burned*)   Here is good news! God has lifted
the barriers between us. According to your penitence, so is
your forgiveness. God accepts you—now, accept one another.
If God loves us, can we not love all others?

Gesture of Reconciliation   (*Embrace persons next to you, nodding heads over one shoulder and then the other, symbolizing
reconciliation.*)

SONG   "Love Is the Answer"

Call to Intercession

LEADER   Believing that more is accomplished by prayer than we can comprehend, we come now to pray for others.

Directed Prayers of Intercession

LEADER   Pray for the person on your left, that you may be one in the spirit, coming to a deep level of understanding, and be workers together for God.

Pray the same for the person on your right.

Pray the same for the person in front of you.

Pray the same for the person behind you.

Pray for any person in the congregation with whom you feel there is a barrier; pray that it might be lifted by love.

Pray for an ever-growing sense of community among the congregations of your denomination.

Pray for a deeper sense of community in this city of pluralism.

Pray for national unity and world community, where mutual respect, love, freedom, and goodwill are offered to all.

RESPONSE   "Threefold Amen" (CONGREGATION *and* CHOIR)

The Vision of the "City of God"

FROM AN ANCIENT LETTER   Revelation 21:1–13, 21–27

FROM AN INCIDENT IN HISTORY   "The City of God"—St. Augustine [12]

FROM A CONTEMPORARY INTERPRETER   "I Have a Dream"—Martin Luther King, Jr.[13]

Our Response

SONG   "Share the Dream" (*This is followed by the Passing of the Peace. As the peace is passed, each worshiper says to another,* "Community begins here. Take peace and joy with you." *Response:* "And with you.")

A MULTIMEDIA PEACE CELEBRATION [14]

Before the Expression—Prelude of Instrumental Music

Where It's At—The Call (*antiphonal reading of* "Go Down Moses" CHOIR, LEADERS, CONGREGATION)

LEADER   When Israel was in Egypt's land,

CHOIR   Let my people go.

LEADER   Oppressed so hard they could not stand,

CHOIR   Let my people go.

CONGREGATION   (*chorus*)

> Go down, Moses,
> Way down in Egypt land,
> Tell ol' Pharaoh,
> Let my people go.

LEADER   When spoke the Lord, bold Moses said—

CHOIR   Let my people go.

LEADER   If not I'll smite your firstborn dead—

CHOIR   Let my people go.

CONGREGATION   (*chorus*)

LEADER   We're moving for peace and that's no jive—

CHOIR   Let my people go.

LEADER   Hear what we're saying—no one can hide—

CHOIR   Let my people go.

CONGREGATION   (*chorus*)

LEADER   The young have decided to work for peace—

CHOIR   Let my people go.

LEADER   What a glorious day for war to cease—

CHOIR   Let my people go.

CONGREGATION   (*chorus*)

LEADER   The oppressed people are on the move—
CHOIR   Let my people go.
LEADER   If you're goin' to be with us you've got to groove—
CHOIR   Let my people go.
CONGREGATION   (*chorus*)

A Shout of Joy—The Praise
FOLK HYMN   "Lord of the Dance" (*with liturgical pantomime*)

Signs of Our Folly—The Confession
• "Neighbors" (*short film*)
• Slides on ecology problem, poor housing, etc.[15]
POEM   "Calvary New Style" [16]

> They nailed Him to a wooden tree,
> The same He bore to Calvary.
> Between two thieves, beneath the sky
> Long years ago did my Lord die.
>
> A man went forth a cause to seek,
> They shot my brother just last week.
> Before the mob could answer, why
> Right in the street we saw him die.
>
> Once more with ignorance and stain
> Another child of God was slain.

UNISON PRAYER   O God, we admit how satisfied we are with our
own action and concerns and how blind we often are to major
human suffering. We are stirred by accounts of war, earth-
quakes, political repression, poverty, hunger—but how quickly
we seek to escape the haunting visions of our suffering brother.
Forgive us for our dullness of spirit and of response. Forgive
us and free us by Your love, which we know in Jesus Christ.
Amen.

The News of Human Freedom—Declaration of Pardon

What Speaks to Us—The Word
THE ANCIENT WORD   Luke 4:16–21; Matthew 25:37–40
THE NOW AND FUTURE WORD   Don't look for me within the morn-

ing sunrise, for you won't find me there . . . don't look for
me within the glow of sunset, you can't hold on to air . . .
Just look for me within the hungry faces within the hungry
eyes. It's there that I am waiting, waiting always, why can't
you realize? Why can't you see the lies, why can't you hear the
cries? Don't look for me behind the smiles of free men, it's easy
sailing then. Don't look for me within the books of history, you
can't change what has been. Just look for me behind the chains
of bondage that bind the souls of men. It's here my heart cries
out for change and justice and you can help my friend. We
can't change what has been but we can start again. Look for
me in the hungry cries of little children, in the eyes that view
a world bewildered by the hate, by a fate they can't comprehend. Don't look for me within the morning glories, that's
not my light you find. Don't look for me in meditation circles,
you can't buy peace of mind. Just open up your eyes and ears
a moment and listen while you can. And you will hear me in
the voices crying and you will understand. When I reach out
in hunger, when I reach out in pain . . . please take my hand.[17]

It's Laid Upon Us—The Commitment

SONG   "Let the World Know"

READER   So the struggles for freedom that remain will be more
strange and difficult than any we have met so far. For we must
struggle for a freedom that enfolds stern justice, stern bravery,
stern love, and simple joy. Blessed art Thou, O Lord our God!
who has confronted us with the necessity of choice and of
creating our own book of Thy Law. How many and how hard
are the choices and the tasks the Almighty has set before us!

UNISON   How much then are we duty bound to struggle, work,
share, give, think, plan, feel, organize, sit-in, speak out, dream,
hope, and be on behalf of mankind! For we must stop the
bloody wars that are killing men and women as we sit here,
disarm the nations of the deadly weapons that threaten to destroy us all, end the poisoning of our planet, make sure that no
one starves, stop brutality in many countries, free the poets

from their jails, educate us all to understand their poetry, liberate us all to explore our inner ecstasies, and encourage and aid us to love one another and share in the human fraternity. All these! [18]

Carry on!—The Commission

LEADER   Go forth as new people—

PEOPLE   Amen!

SONG   "Ain't Goin' To Study War No More" [19]
(*verses*)

Goin' to lay down my sword and shield. . . .
Goin' to put on my walking shoes. . . .
Goin' to seek the truth in this world. . . .
Goin' to work to liberate all men.

FESTIVAL OF LIGHTS

Explanation: Worshipers will gather in worship area. Chairs will be arranged in a circle with the altar in the center. A large white candle representing Christ, the Light of the World, will decorate the altar. Each worshiper will be given a candle as he enters the room.

Introduction

LEADER   One of the happiest, prettiest and most widely celebrated festivals in India is *Diwali* (*pronounced* Dee-wal-lee) —the Festival of Lights. It is akin to our Christmas and New Year's celebrations with some Thanksgiving thrown in. Families gather together, houses are cleaned, food is shared with poor families, and merchants open a new fiscal year.

Their autumn holiday commemorates the end of the rains and gives thanks for a good harvest. Participants light tiny cotton wicks in clay saucers filled with oil to guide the harvest for another year of plenty. The lights are placed on rivers and on the ledges of houses and walls in every village.

Christians also join in this colorful holiday, recognizing it as a symbol of "Jesus, the Light of the World." (*Light center candle.*)

LEADER   God lights up men's hearts when they truly hear with the inner ear and see with the eyes of faith. Let us now open ourselves to receive God's light.

HYMN   "Light of the World, We Hail Thee" (*verses 1, 2, and 3*)

SCRIPTURE   Matthew 5:14–17

Prayer

LEADER   Dear God, we go out into a night that is growing dark, but in the sky are countless stars.

PEOPLE   Give us light.

LEADER   We live at the edge of ghettos that are bleak. But in them are children playing and laughing.

PEOPLE   Give us hope.

LEADER   The spirit of the poor seems gravely broken, yet, now they march upon the treasury of the earth.

PEOPLE   Give us courage.

LEADER   Young men are bleeding and dying in the East; still we give thanks for dialogue in the West.

PEOPLE   Give us peace.

LEADER   The old structures bind us like Gulliver while students of the world demand change.

PEOPLE   Give us wisdom.

LEADER   All things once so strong and sure seem to be passing, and, behold new things everywhere!

PEOPLE   Give us faith.

LEADER   Tonight, O God, we celebrate a great mystery, for a sign of Thy grace has marked this place and Your promise like a rainbow is seen among us. Amen.[20]

THE CHURCH OF THE LAMPS [21]

When the sun has set and darkness has fallen, the lamps are lighted in the quaint white houses of a little village in southern Europe. There is darkness only in the gray stone church that stands on the summit of a hill overlooking the town. This church is called "The House of Many Lamps."

Legend says that this "House of Many Lamps" was built long ago in the sixteenth century by an old duke. He had several beautiful daughters whom he loved devotedly. He dreaded to have them marry and leave home, for, said he, "Each one has her place and the house is lonely in some spot without her."

As the duke grew old he began to wonder what he might leave behind him to perpetuate his memory. Finally he decided to build a church so beautiful that men would worship as soon as they entered because it would draw them to God. He drew up the plans for the building and watched eagerly as the work proceeded.

At last the day came when all was finished, and the duke took one of his daughters to see it. She admired the simple lines, the carving, and the stained-glass windows.

"But, Father," she said, "where are the lamps to hang?"

"There will be no hanging lamps, my daughter," he replied. "Each worshiper will carry his own lamp. I have provided small bronze lamps—one for every person in the village up to the number the church will hold."

Then he added, more slowly, "Some corner of God's house will be dark and lonely if all His sons and daughters do not come to worship Him at the appointed time." And these words were carved in the stone over the doorway.

The years have passed. The bronze lamps have been handed down from father to son and carefully treasured. When the sweet-toned bell of the old church rings, the village people wend their way up the hill, each carrying his own lamp. The church is always filled, for no family wishes its corner to be dark and gloomy.

LEADER   Each of you has a light to carry, to penetrate the darkness of the world. Jesus said, "Let your light so shine before men, that they may see your good works and give glory to your Father." By your light and the light of other Christians, evil will be exposed, crime will flee, goodness will be stimulated, healing and growth will result, and the whole world will be led to God. Take the light you receive in Christ back to your home, your church, your community and let it shine for all to see. (*Leader lights candle from the central candle. All other lights will be out.*)

LEADER   You will all symbolically receive the Light of the World and pass that light to your neighbor.

SOLO   "Light One Little Candle" (SOLOIST *sings until all candles are lit.*)

Benediction

LEADER   May the winds never dim the flame that has been lit in your heart. Amen.

(*After benediction, all will depart in silence, taking their lighted candles.*)

CELEBRATING SERVANTHOOD [22]

OPENING SONG   "Kumbayah"

Litany of Service

LEADER   We pause just now to think about those who are sick, hungry, deeply troubled, unemployed, stranded, poor, lonely, mentally confused, and burdened in other ways.

RESPONSE   We remember One who had compassion upon the sorrowful, wept with the lonely, healed the sick, took time to assist those in trouble, and stirred people up to good works.

May we, His followers, not be content to sit out our Christian lives on cushioned pews.

LEADER   In the light of our Christian calling to servanthood, we would evaluate our jobs and opportunities, and the ways to help the refugee, the unemployed, the alcoholic, the orphan, the unmarried mother, the victims of tragedies, and the physically handicapped.

RESPONSE   O God, make us like our Master—a servant to neighbors, shepherd to the straying, comforter of the sorrowful, protector of the weak and helpless.

LEADER   May we not be content only to meet physical or mental needs. Also help us to minister to the deep, unuttered yearnings of peoples' souls.

RESPONSE   Thus, O Lord, may we demonstrate Your love in our serving, so that those we serve may sense a purpose that makes life significant and the God of life, good.

Call to Prayer   "People of Peace, Children of Love"

Moment of Silent Meditation

Reading of the Scriptures

OLD TESTAMENT   Hosea 11:4—"God Yearns for His Wayward People"

NEW TESTAMENT   Matthew 22:34–40—"The Great Commandment"

Sermon   "What the World Needs Now"

HYMN   "What the World Needs Now Is Love Sweet Love"

Call to Share

I WONDER . . .
  Why some people are white and some are brown?
  Why some people live in big houses and some have no homes at all?
  Why can't all boys and girls have as much fun as I do?
I WONDER . . .
  Do I have better clothes and toys and food than other boys because I am better?

Or am I any better because I have more?
What makes the difference—anyway?
I WONDER . . .
If no one had ever given me anything, or
If no one cared for me, or
If I didn't have a home, food, clothes, a church and a school
    What kind of a boy would I be?
    What kind of a man could I become?
I WONDER . . .
If God doesn't expect me to share with others?
If God doesn't expect all Christians to share?
If maybe that isn't a reason we have so much?
I KNOW . . .
That I will be happier if I do share,
    and
That my sharing will help boys and girls in other lands
    to hear about Christ and be happier.
I WONDER . . .
Why any Christian wouldn't want to share?
And I do mean really share—not just the leftover crumbs,
    but a real Christian portion.
I WONDER . . .
How Christian we really are? [23]

Offering of Selves for Service

Open your eyes and see . . .
    the juvenile delinquents seeking recognition and someone to care;
    the neighbor that carries a heavy load and needs someone to listen;
    the one who works at the desk next to yours and irritates you but
        needs to be understood;
    the ballot that must be studied and stamped;
    the community issues that need your influence;
    the lonely widow who used to be in your crowd;
    the missionary on foreign soil who, at times, draws on your strength;
    the dope addict, racked with pain,
        the alcoholic,
            the prisoner,
                the prostitute

who need to know that there is a place for them in God's plan. Lord, give us the courage to give our life for others—as You did. In the name of Him, whom to love is to be involved. Amen.

Offering of Monies for Service

Doxology and Prayer

Commitment in Communion

INVITATION AND PRAYER

DISTRIBUTION   (*Each person serves his neighbor, using whatever words he chooses.*)

Passing of the Peace

The Dismissal   To each of you here, I appoint you a missionary for Jesus Christ. To all who so dedicate their lives, I remind you a missionary in today's world is a world citizen—one who does not let man-made barriers of race, class, or nation separate him from fellow humans. He or she is at home anywhere. Where there is need, he seeks to be of service. Where there is fragmentation, he seeks to be God's agent of reconciliation. Where there is injustice, he seeks to be God's revolutionary agent for change. Sometimes his service is silent, but he must always be ready to speak the "why" and to interpret aloud his action so that the world may be confronted and know that there, in this time and place, God is at work.

Within your life is a miracle. Go—live your faith.

CELEBRATION THROUGH RHYTHM

Call to Explain

LEADER   We are here to celebrate the joy of being alive! To express our feelings! To let ourselves go! So, you are invited to sway, sing, shout! To become involved as your emotions lead you!

Rhythm involves a person physically, mentally, spiritually, totally!

LET GO! LET GO! in praise to God.

Call to Prayer

LEADER   "HELP ME TO SPEAK OUT"

> God, I want to speak out,
>   To be free to express myself
>   in words, or paint, or music.
> But I can't!
> Oh, I'm physically free—
>   But emotionally tied up.
> Help me, Lord, to be able to speak,
>   To be honest and open about myself and my world,
>   To not be afraid that someone may laugh—or cry.
> O God, through Thy love may I be free also to love;
>   And therefore free
>   to speak,
>   or paint,
>   or sing,
>   or write,
>   or dance.
>   Amen.

Call to Sing   "Lord of the Dance"

Call to Listen   2 Samuel 6:5, 12–14, 15; Psalms 66:1, 2; 95:1–3; 97:1–8; 150:1–6. (*Worshipers are told to express their feelings in creative gestures as the Scriptures are read.*)

Call to Express—Expressions of Joy in Life [24]

Call to Go

LEADER

> Go now,
>   Scatter into the world.

Be enthusiastic—joyful—
Pass the peace—God loves you!

SONG "When the Saints Go Marching In" (*Worshipers sing as they march around, joyfully shaking hands with others, swaying in rhythm—then depart when music is over.*)

CELEBRATION IN SONG [25]

Instruments: guitars, harmonica, drums, flute, tambourine

Prelude "Early in the Morning" (*Instrumental*)

Call to Worship "The Times They Are A-Changin'" (LEADER *chants each line, followed by the* CHOIR *or* ENSEMBLE *singing the line.*)

INVOCATION "Kumbayah" (LEADER *sings a verse, then all* WORSHIPERS *sing that verse. Continue with all verses.*)

HYMN OF PRAISE "Amen" (CONGREGATION *standing and singing.*)

Confession of Sin

ACKNOWLEDGMENT OF OUR CORPORATE CONDITION "Eve of Destruction" (*Words spoken in unison by all* WORSHIPERS, *then all sing the song.*)

ACKNOWLEDGMENT OF OUR PERSONAL CONDITION "The Sounds of Silence" (*Recording or solo*—WORSHIPERS *kneel with bowed head as song is played*)

Absolution WORDS OF POSSIBILITY "Blowin' in the Wind" (CHOIR, QUARTET, *or* ENSEMBLE *singing*)

The Old Testament Lesson

WORD FROM THE WORD I   "Samson and Delilah" (MINISTER *chanting lines with congregation responding antiphonally; or can be a bass solo.*)

WORD FROM THE WORLD   "Clouds Above" (*soprano solo*)

The New Testament Lesson

WORD FROM THE WORD II   "The Wedding Banquet" (*duet*)

WORD FROM THE WORLD   "Look What You've Done" (*choir*)

Sermon   "There's a World Out There" (*The* MINISTER *sings verses, assisted by the* ENSEMBLE *or* CHOIR. *Between verses, he elaborates with brief homilies or illustrations of the thoughts conveyed in the song.*)

Credo   STATEMENT OF FAITH AND DEDICATION "Bridge Over Troubled Waters" (*everyone singing*)

PASTORAL PRAYER   "Let It Be" (*choir*); "Last Night I Had the Strangest Dream" (*solo by* MINISTER *or* LEADER)

Offertory   "Let Us Break Bread Together" (*everyone singing*); "Sons of God" (*everyone singing*)

HYMN OF DEDICATION   "If I Had a Hammer" (*everyone singing*)

ADMONITION   "Put Your Hand in the Hand" (*choir*)

Benediction   "Amen, Amen, Amen, Amen" (*everyone singing*)

Postlude   Coffee and Songs

Section 3

FESTIVAL OCCASIONS

Section 3

FESTIVAL
OCCASIONS

ADVENT WREATH LIGHTING

These brief ceremonies may be used as a part of the church worship for the four pre-Christmas Sundays, and also as a lighting of a wreath in each family's home. The wreath should be at least two to three feet in diameter, with four candles securely placed.

Lighting the First Advent Candle (*Fourth Sunday before Christmas*)

INTRODUCTORY SENTENCES Today is the beginning of Advent, the preparation time for celebrating Christ's birth and the Christian insights into God and life. As the prophet Isaiah said, "For behold, darkness shall cover the earth, and thick darkness the peoples; but the Lord will arise upon you, and his glory will be seen upon you."

SCRIPTURE READINGS Therefore thus says the Lord, the God of Israel, concerning the shepherds who care for my people: "You have scattered my flock, and have driven them away, and you have not attended to them. Behold, I will attend to you for your evil doings, says the Lord. Then I will gather the rem-

70

nant of my flock out of all the countries where I have driven them, and I will bring them back to their fold, and they shall be fruitful and multiply. I will set shepherds over them who will care for them, and they shall fear no more, nor be dismayed, neither shall any be missing, says the Lord.

"Behold, the days are coming, says the Lord, when I will raise up for David a righteous Branch, and he shall reign as king and deal wisely, and shall execute justice and righteousness in the land. In his days Judah will be saved, and Israel will dwell securely. And this is the name by which he will be called: 'The Lord is our righteousness'" (Jeremiah 23:2–6; or one of the following: Genesis 12:1–9; Zechariah 10:6–12; Romans 13:8–10; Hebrews 11:8–16; Matthew 21:1–13; Mark 13:32–37; Luke 1:26–33.)

HYMN "Song and Dance"

PRAYER (*while lighting the first candle*) As we light this first Advent candle, we begin our anticipation of Christ's birthday celebration. We light the flame of hope in our hearts. We will strive to make this a season of joy that places Christ in the center of what we do. We want this candle to remind us of Christ and our commitment to His Kingdom.

O God, make ready for Your rule, the kingdom of this world and our hearts. Come rapidly and save us, so that violence and crying will be no more, and righteousness and peace may bless Your children, through Jesus Christ our Lord. Amen.

Lighting the Second Advent Candle (*Third Sunday before Christmas*)

INTRODUCTORY SENTENCE We are here to light the second Advent candle, "The Kingdom of heaven is near. . . . Get the Lord's road ready for him, make a straight path for him to travel! . . . Turn away from your sins . . ." (Matthew 3:2 TEV).

SCRIPTURE READINGS

But you, O Bethlehem Ephrathah,
    who are little to be among the clans of Judah,

from you shall come forth for me
  one who is to be ruler in Israel,
whose origin is from of old,
  from ancient days.
Therefore he shall give them up until the time
  when she who is in travail has brought forth;
then the rest of his brethren shall return
  to the people of Israel.
And he shall stand and feed his flock in the strength of
  the Lord, in the majesty of the name of the Lord his God.
And they shall dwell secure for now he shall be great
  to the ends of the earth.

Micah 5:2–4

(Or you may substitute one of the following: Isaiah 33:17–22; Genesis 15:1–15; Romans 13:11–14; 9:1–8; Matthew 25:14–29; John 3:1–17.)

HYMN "Don't Wait for an Angel" or "O Come, O Come Emmanuel"

PRAYER (*while lighting the second candle*) We light this candle to remind us how the way is to be prepared for Jesus' coming. We pray that as Advent light is increased, our readiness may also increase.

O God, who prepared of old the minds and hearts of man for the coming of Thy Son, and whose Spirit ever works to illumine our darkened lives with the light of the gospel, prepare now our minds and hearts, we pray, so that Christ may dwell within us, and ever reign in our thoughts and affections as the King of Love and the Prince of Peace. Amen.

Lighting the Third Advent Candle (*Second Sunday before Christmas*)

INTRODUCTORY SENTENCE We come today to light the third Advent candle. "Ho, everyone who thirsts, come to the waters; and he who has no money, come, buy and eat! Come, buy wine and milk without money and without price" (Isaiah 55:1).

SCRIPTURE READINGS

The people who walked in darkness
  have seen a great light;

those who dwelt in a land of deep darkness,
    on them has light shined.

Isaiah 9:2

For to us a child is born,
    to us a son is given;
and the government will be upon his shoulder,
    and his name will be called
"Wonderful Counselor, Mighty God,
    Everlasting Father, Prince of Peace."
Of the increase of his government and of peace
    there will be no end,
upon the throne of David, and over his kingdom,
    to establish it, and to uphold it
with justice and with righteousness
from this time forth and for evermore.
The zeal of the Lord of hosts will do this.

Isaiah 9:6, 7

(Or one of the following may be substituted: Jeremiah 33:14–16; Genesis 28:10–22; 1 Corinthians 3:18–4:5; 1 John 5:1–5; Matthew 3:1–11; 11:2–10.)

HYMN "Let All Mortal Flesh Keep Silence" or "Hurry Lord, Come Quickly"

PRAYER (*while lighting the third candle*) We are halfway to Christmas. As we light this candle may our preparation for Him be quickened. May we be saved from being overly absorbed in the materialism and commercialization of the season, so that our hearts will be filled with the spirit and hope of Christ.

O Lord God, keep us watchful for ways that we might ready the world and ourselves for Your rule. May we be strengthened and directed by the assurance of Your love and Your Holy Spirit, in Jesus' Name. Amen.

Lighting the Fourth Advent Candle (*One Sunday before Christmas*)

INTRODUCTORY SENTENCE We come on this last Sunday before Christmas to light the fourth Advent candle. "How beautiful upon the mountains are the feet of him who brings good tidings, who publishes peace, who brings good tidings of good, who publishes salvation, who says to Zion, 'Your God reigns' " (Isaiah 52:7).

SCRIPTURE READINGS In the beginning was the Word, and the Word was with God, and the Word was God. He was in the beginning with God; all things were made through him, and without him was not anything made that was made. In him was life, and the life was the light of men. The light shines in the darkness, and the darkness has not overcome it.

There was a man sent from God, whose name was John. He came for testimony, to bear witness to the light, that all might believe through him. He was not the light, but came to bear witness to the light.

The true light that enlightens every man was coming into the world. He was in the world, and the world was made through him, yet the world knew him not. He came to his own home, and his own people received him not. But to all who received him, who believed in his name, he gave power to become children of God; who were born, not of blood nor of the will of the flesh nor of the will of man, but of God.

And the Word became flesh and dwelt among us, full of grace and truth; we have beheld his glory, glory as of the only Son from the Father (John 1:1–14).

(Or substitute one of the following: Jeremiah 23:3–8; 1 Samuel 1:21–28; Philippians 4:4–7; Galatians 3:23–29; Luke 1:26–38; 38–56.)

HYMN "Now Thank We All Our God" or "Joy to the World"

PRAYER (*while lighting the fourth candle*) We bring our Advent wreath to full blaze in hope that we may see clearly all that is made known to us in the coming of Christ.

Eternal God our Father: through long generations You prepared a way in our world for the coming of Your Son. By Your Spirit You are still bringing the light of the gospel to darkened lives. May we be sufficiently prepared to be able to welcome

Jesus Christ to rule our thoughts and claim our love, as Lord
of Lords and King of Kings, to whom be glory forever. Amen.

HANGING OF THE GREENS [1]

Explanation *This service is planned for decorating the sanctuary
prior to Christmas in the midst of worship. Sunday school classes
are used, with a family representative hanging a decorating
piece. The major decorating should be done in advance, with
only a specified number of pieces added equaling the number
of classes. During the course of the service, representatives of
each class leave their places to hang the greens. Either the various
graded choirs or Sunday school departments sing. Adults and
youth read the Scriptures. Following the service, a tasting party
is held where all classes or women's groups have provided Christmas goodies. This service takes immense organization; however,
herein is the secret of its beauty, meaning, and participation.*

Musical Introduction
ORCHESTRA   Medley of Christmas Music
CARILLON MUSIC   "Let All Mortal Flesh Keep Silence"
ORGAN PRELUDE   "Silent Night" (*During this number the can-
dles are lit.*)
PROCESSIONAL HYMN   "O Come, All Ye Faithful"

Call to Worship and Invocation
THE PROPHECY   Isaiah 9:2–7

Hanging of the Greens   (*Families from classes hang decorations.*)
ANTHEM   "Break Forth O Beauteous Heavenly Light"—Bach
THE ANNUNCIATION   Luke 1:26–33

Hanging of the Greens   (*Families from classes hang decorations.*)
CAROL   "Angels We Have Heard on High"—Youth Choir (*Congregation joins in singing first verse.*)
THE MAGNIFICAT   Luke 1:45–55

Hanging of the Greens   (*Families from classes hang decorations.*)
CAROL   "Deck the Halls"—Junior Choir
THE FULFILLMENT   Luke 2:1–20

Hanging of the Greens   (*Families from classes hang decorations.*)
CAROL   "Little Baby Jesus"—Cherub Choir

The Evening Prayer   Eternal God, who has declared love to all men through the birth and life of Jesus Christ, our hearts are filled with gratitude for all that this season brings. We are mindful of the stars that shed light upon the earth and bear us back in memory to Bethlehem, and the carols that fill the air retelling the story of a humble manger where our Saviour was born. May these decorations of wreaths, bells, ribbons, and banners, which we have hung tonight for eyes to see, give glory to the Prince of Peace. Grant, O Father, that His love of peace, His faith in things unseen, His pity for the poor, His actions of love, His vision of the coming age shall find room in the inn of our hearts. So may we live at peace with one another and with all Your family, through the Spirit of Jesus Christ the Lord. Amen.

Hanging of the Greens   (*Families from classes hang decorations.*)
CAROL   "What Child Is This?"—Children's Choir
ANTHEM   "Gloria in Excelsis"—Sanctuary Choir

Meditation   "Behind Our Christmas Traditions" The true Christmas story centers in the Christ Child, but it began long before that. It is a story that has changed with the passing of history and the transforming power of human experiences. Each generation of mankind adds and subtracts to the pattern of the story. Let us see why we now follow certain traditions and customs when we celebrate Christmas today.

Our story goes back to at least 4,000 years ago and possibly longer than that. It begins in Mesopotamia, called the cradle of civilization. Here Christmas really began as the festival which renewed the world for another year. Here began the "twelve days" of Christmas, the festivals, the bright fires, the giving of gifts, the carnivals, merrymakings and clownings, the mummers who sang and played from house to house, the church processions with their lights and songs. All these and more began centuries before Christ was born. And they celebrated the arrival of a New Year.

All peoples all over the world learned from Mesopotamia. Everything happening there was in the course of time imitated by its neighbors—imitated, yet never copied exactly. Thus it changed its face as it went. One road traveled through Greece to Rome and another road led from Asia Minor through the Balkans, up the Danube Valley into the heart of Europe.

The Northland peoples knew that winter followed summer, and that spring followed winter, and that winter was the time when all nature's green life died except in the evergreens. All the Northland cherished the evergreen that did not die. Thus long before the Christian era, evergreens were used as an emblem of eternal life.

Holly was symbolic of joy and peace, and primitive people would hang it over their doors in the form of wreaths to entice spirits to bring good luck. Why a circle? Because a circle is the symbol of timelessness, and the green leaves of life everlasting.

According to some sources, Christ's crown of thorns had been fashioned from holly leaves. At first its berries were white, but when the crown was pressed down on His brow, blood drops turned the berries a bright red.

Because holly was originally regarded as magic, it was believed that if a house were hung at Christmas with thorny holly, the husband would rule throughout the year; if hung with smooth holly, the woman would be master.

Since mistletoe grows as a parasite at the top of trees, it was symbolic of the link between heaven and earth to the ancient people. The Druids believed that it contained a sacred spirit. Priests dressed in long flowing robes marched into the forest followed by men, women, and children. Trumpets were sounded and bards chanted as they approached the sacred oak trees upon which the mistletoe grew. The high priest carried a gold curved knife with which he cut down the mistletoe. He threw it down to young beautiful girls who caught the sprigs in a sparkling white cloth. The mistletoe was not allowed to touch the earth or it would bring bad luck. The priest then gave to everyone a sprig to hang over their doors at home, and all who entered received a "kiss of peace."

Among the Romans, the mistletoe was also considered a symbol of hope and peace. Therefore, when enemies met under it, they laid aside their weapons, kissed each other, and declared a truce until the next day.

Where did we get our Christmas tree and when did it arrive? Giving reverence to green trees in the dead of winter and decorating them goes so far back into antiquity that we cannot trace the origin. The early Egyptians took green date palms into their homes significant of "life triumphant over death," and when the ancient pagans of the Northland were converted to Christianity, the evergreen tree came to denote His bringing new life to the world after the long days of winter.

Martin Luther is credited with putting lights on the Christmas tree. The story goes that he was walking home through a forest one night. He was so impressed by the beautiful stars in the winter sky and by the stately evergreens that he tried to explain all the glory to his family when he arrived home. Words failed him, so he went out and cut a small fir tree and placed lighted candles on it to represent the starry sky above the stable the night that Christ was born.

Did you know that there was once a real Santa Claus? He was born St. Nicholas late in the third century of Christian parents, and died December 6 in the fourth century. When he was a very young man, he decided to devote his life to Christian service. He was such a remarkable person that many varied and numerous legends have been gathered about his life on earth, and his life as a saint after his death. Although his job in America comes but once a year, his work in Europe and Asia lasts all year round. In fact, he is probably the hardest working saint of all. All over the world, sailors and travelers, and even countries revere and honor him, and he is patron saint. Most countries celebrate his memory December 6 with exchange of gifts.

One of Nicholas's chief characteristics was his unsurpassed generosity. He soon learned how many people were oppressed with poverty, and he often went out in disguise and distributed presents, especially to children. Thus he became the patron saint of children everywhere. His fame spread far and wide all over the world and so today it is good that the memory of generous St. Nicholas is still alive for he brings happiness to millions of children.

The true Christmas story centers in the birth of Christ depicted by the nativity scene. This is a Christmas custom that St. Francis of Assisi made popular.

During the Middle Ages there were very few books, and even if there had been more, people could not read them. Church ceremonies were conducted in Latin, so that Christmas had little meaning for many who attended. This worried St. Francis, for he wanted to humanize the teaching of the Scriptures and to show his followers that Christ also came from humble beginnings. So he assembled the necessary properties—a manger, star, a live ox, and a donkey. Real persons took the parts of Mary, Joseph, and the shepherds. St. Francis arranged the scene and placed a life-size wax figure of the Christ Child in the manger. For the first time many understood the true meaning of the Christmas story. As they stood before the manger, the good saint led his people in songs of praises to the Christ Child and from his "jovial singing" came a new idea about the holiday season—the singing of Christmas carols. Everyone was so impressed by the Christmas ceremony and the singing of the carols that the rites were repeated year after year and soon the custom spread through the world.

Only a few of the customs and traditions that we observe today have been mentioned here. All these and many more have come to us from our historic past. In this moment of time in which we are living, we are a part of that past, the past which brings to us the finest traditions of men and women who have given to Christmas their deepest and enduring selves. Christmas is an expression of a faith and hope which for generations have answered death with a song of triumph. After thousands of years the festival that has grown about the birth of the Christ Child remains an affirmation that all things can be made anew.
CAROL "Joy to the World"—All

Benediction (CONGREGATION *remain seated.*)
CAROL OF DISMISSAL "Lord, Dismiss Us With Thy Blessing" (*medley of carols as congregation is ushered out one row at a time starting from the rear—tasting party follows*)

CHRISTMAS BIRTHDAY CELEBRATION

Explanation *This service is designed for a Sunday Christmas though it can be used also on Christmas Eve. A huge birthday cake is the center focus. The cake should be four (4) feet across, with three (3) or four (4) layers, upon which are placed twenty (20) candles—one (1) for each century. The cake is made of containers, or cardboard, decorated with frosting. To each* WORSHIPER *as he enters the sanctuary, the* USHERS *give a serpentine, a colorful crepe stole, and the program bulletin. Two communion tables should be placed at the sides with the loaf and cup (some may want to use the cake as a symbol of bread). Offering trays are placed at the side of the cake.*

Gathering Music (*medley of traditional or contemporary Christmas carols*)

PROCESSIONAL HYMN "O, Come All Ye Faithful" or "Song and Dance"

The Greeting

LEADER We are here to celebrate the birthday of Jesus Christ!

RESPONSE Blessed be God, our Eternal Friend!

LEADER This is a happy occasion, because our lives have been enlightened by Jesus.

RESPONSE Praise God, from whom the gift has come.

Invocation

LEADER Thanks be to Thee, O God, for Jesus Christ! With humble, reverent hearts we acknowledge the light He has brought to illuminate our darkness. We thank Thee for what He revealed of Your love and purposes; and for the insistent challenge that lures the best in us. Enter now the thresholds of our lives with some invasion of insight, faith, and power. May the miracle of Christmas happen here, inspiring us with the promise of peace and the victory of righteousness through Jesus Christ. Amen.

SOLO "The Birthday of the King"

The Events Surrounding His Birth "Christmas According to Joseph" (*sermon in the first person*) [2]

CAROL "Angels, From the Realms of Glory" or "The First Christmas"

Lighting of the Birthday Cake

LEADER Jesus has meant so much to our world, collectively and personally. Let us recall His contributions that light up our world: (*One candle is lit as each benefit is mentioned. Two* ASSISTANTS *will light the candles. The* CHOIR *will chant an* "Amen" *or* "Hallelujah" *after each. Lights are dimmed for candlelighting.*)

LEADER Jesus has shown us love. (*Amen*) Jesus has shown us God. (*Amen*) Jesus has shown us what an authentic person really is. (*Amen*) Jesus has given womanhood a new dignity. (*Amen*) Jesus has given all people an infinite worth. (*Amen*) Jesus has changed forever the human outlook. (*Amen*) Jesus has quickened the conscience of the status quo. (*Amen*) Jesus has given us a new code for living. (*Amen*) Jesus has broken the barriers down between people. (*Amen*) Jesus has reconciled man to God. (*Amen*) Jesus has given a power to break the chains of evil habits. (*Amen*) Jesus has brought freedom to life. (*Amen*) Jesus has given hope to existence. (*Amen*) Jesus has given purpose for life. (*Amen*) Jesus died for us in defeating the evils of men. (*Amen*) Jesus was raised vindicating the true way. (*Amen*) Jesus proved love is stronger than hate, and that good will outlast evil. (*Amen*) Jesus promises us life eternal and abundant if we follow Him faithfully. (*Amen*) Jesus is the Way. (*Amen*) Jesus is the Truth. (*Amen*) Jesus is the Life. (*Amen*)

The Influence of That One Life   He was born in a village stable. No birth could be lowlier. Possessed of profound wisdom, he had but meager education. No wife, no child—he showed each lonely heart its deepest need.

For thirty years, near the village of his birth, he grew and learned his simple trade, shaping the native wood to serve the wants of home and craft.

Three years he wandered, teaching, shaping the native hearts to service of truth and love. He was never more than a few hundred miles from his home.

He held no earthly rank or office, wrote no book, no song, painted no picture, builded no monument.

His native land was ruled by conquerors and foreign legions. While still in the flush of youth, his own people turned against this man who strangely taught that evil can only be overcome by good.

He was denied by his close friend, deserted by most, betrayed for thirty pieces of silver by one he had befriended.

One dark hour he knelt in the garden, his hour of decision. He gave himself over to his enemies, was tried and condemned in mockery, spat upon and lashed, nailed to a cross between two thieves.

He died asking forgiveness for his persecutors while his executioners gambled for his only earthly possession—his robe. He was laid in a borrowed tomb.

Nearly two thousand years have passed and none has reigned or wrought, or served, or dreamed who has so touched and molded human life. He is the ideal—the example—who has inspired the noblest and the humblest lives—the great unalterable, wholesome, growing influence in a world of blood and tears.

He who was friendless would be friend of all. Homeless, he dwells in countless homes. Books on his life fill libraries. His gospels cover the earth. Scholars, illiterates, rich men, beggars, rulers, and slaves, all are measured by his life.

But this one solitary life surpasses all in power. Its influence is the one remaining and sustaining hope of future years.

In a Roman court nearly twenty centuries ago Pontius Pilate asked of the multitude demanding the death of this young Galilean:

"I find no evil in him—What shall I do with this man?" Today each troubled heart must meet the challenge when the Pilate within asks:

WHAT SHALL I DO . . . ? [3]

CHOIR "Noel, Noel, Noel"

What He Has Meant to Me Personally (*three three-minute testimonies*)

Prayer of Confession

LEADER O God, have mercy upon us for treating so shabbily our Lord. Forgive our misunderstandings, our prejudices of race and rank, color and nation, and the hatreds we have allowed to divide us. Break down the barriers, we pray, so that the Spirit of Jesus Christ may find lodging in the inner room of our hearts, and in our world. Thank You Lord, for Thy forgiveness. Amen.

CAROL "Hark the Herald Angels Sing"

Presentation of Birthday Gifts   (*Explanation: Money for Jesus'*
Kingdom is brought by WORSHIPERS *in the most colorful envelopes*
possible. Effort is made to encourage each WORSHIPER *to give a*
certain amount for each year of Christ's influence, i.e., $1.00 *to*
$10.00 *per year.* WORSHIPERS *will come forward to place their*
gifts beside the cake where trays are placed—then proceed to the
side where communion tables contain the emblems. They will
break off a piece of bread, dip it in the chalice, then form a
large circle around the sanctuary.)

Words of Invitation
LEADER   Remember the words of our Lord Jesus, how He said,
   "It is more blessed to give than to receive."
PRAISE SONG   "Happy Birthday, Dear Jesus"

Offertory Prayer
LEADER   O Lord, may these gifts we bring bless Your holy Name.
   Grant that they may represent sufficient love and sacrifice to
   be acceptable in Thy sight, for Christ's sake. Amen.

Presenting Gifts   (CONGREGATION *goes forward one man at a*
time.)

Sharing the Eucharist   (*Each* WORSHIPER *serves himself at one*
of the communion tables, after placing gift upon the altar.)
LEADER   "Taste and see that the Lord is good!" Whatever you
   do, in work or deed, do everything in the Name of the Lord
   Jesus, giving thanks to God the Father through Him.
CAROL   "Joy to the World" or "Shout for Joy" (*While in circle,*
singing, WORSHIPERS *throw serpentines or balloons to express*
joy.)

Shalom   (WORSHIPERS *are invited to dining-fellowship with cake*
and punch.)

LENTEN FESTIVAL

This service may be held at a Family Night Dinner or on Sunday morning.

THE PROCESSIONAL "Come, Let Us Sing"

The Call to Worship

LEADER "Behold, I stand at the door and knock. . . ."

PEOPLE How was that again?

LEADER "Behold, I stand at the door and knock."

PEOPLE What is that supposed to mean?

LEADER Well, it is another way of saying that God is always seeking us.

PEOPLE And if He is seeking us, and has found us, what then?

LEADER We are the objects of God's search, but we are persons, not things. We must respond, yet God does not force us.

PEOPLE You mean that the first step, then, is from God? And the second step—the response—is something *we* have to do?

LEADER Right! And this is what worship is about: to open doors through which the Spirit of God may move, so that we can respond.

PEOPLE Well, let's go ahead then! Let's be open to God's Spirit —and then respond!

Remembering the Needs of Our Community

LEADER This is a time of remembering . . .

PEOPLE . . . a time of remembering those of our community who are struggling, who are searching, who are in need.

LEADER O God, help us think of those among us who . . .

PEOPLE . . . are struggling with personal problems, like loneli-

ness, anxiety, a need for self-discipline, problems with money
or in their marriage, a desire to do better in school. We are
concerned for those.

LEADER   O God, help us think of those among us who . . .

PEOPLE   . . . are searching for more love in their lives, both to
give and to receive; who are in need of patience and understanding in their dealings with themselves and those around
them; who are hoping to develop more honesty and fairness
in their relationships with others. We are thinking about these
today.

LEADER   O God, help us think of those among us who . . .

PEOPLE   . . . need God; who want to be closer to Him; who
need a deeper commitment in every area of their lives; who
want to improve their devotional lives; who search for a real
purpose—God's purpose—in their lives; who are trying to set
their priorities straight by searching right now for God's will
for them in their lives. Our Lord, we reach out.

ALL   We reach out in response to Your searching love that seeks
the center of our hearts and lives. We gather here to remember
our needs and to respond to Your offer of Yourself as the best
answer for our problems. Amen.

THE HYMN OF HOPE   "Here We Are"

The Affirmation of Faith

LEADER   Let us say what we believe.
PEOPLE

> I believe in the living God,
>   the Father of mankind,
>   who creates and sustains the universe
>   by His power and in His love.
> I believe in Jesus Christ,
>   the Man of Nazareth;
>   because of His words and work,
>   His way with others,
>   His use of suffering,
>   His conquest of death,

I know what human life ought to be and what God
is like
I believe that the Spirit of God is
present with us, now and always,
and can be experienced
in prayer, in forgiveness,
in the Word, the sacraments,
in the fellowship of the church,
and in all we do. Amen.[4]

From VENTURES IN WORSHIP edited by David James Randolph. Copyright
© 1969 by Abingdon Press.

The Gloria
THE SCRIPTURE   Ephesians 4:11–32

The Pastoral Prayer   Lord God, it is all too easy for us to take
Your gift of life and love for granted, and to assume You owe
us the privilege. Help us as the Lenten season begins, to
remember what it cost You to trust us in this way. We can only
guess at the pain and grief we cause You by our shallow,
senseless rationalizations and the lip service we give Your ideals.
Forgive us for the way we treat one another. We believe the
cross of Jesus is the measure both of our shame and of Your love.
Help us to keep the price of our redemption before us. Deepen
our understanding. Cause us to deny and sacrifice ourselves, thus
to identify with Jesus and the cross. So may we be more ready
to serve, whatever the cost, in the Spirit of Jesus Christ. Amen.

The Lord's Prayer
THE PRAYER HYMN   "A Song for Lent"

The Words of Thanksgiving
MINISTER   O God our Father, the fountain of all goodness, who
has been gracious to us through all the years of our
life: we give thanks for Your lovingkindness which
has filled our days and brought us to this time and
place.
RESPONSE   We praise Your holy name, O Lord.
MINISTER   You have given us life and reason, and set us in the

world which is full of Your glory. You have comforted us with family and friends and ministered to us through the hands and minds of our fellows.

RESPONSE   We praise Your holy name, O Lord.

MINISTER   You have set in our hearts a hunger for Yourself and given us Your peace. You have redeemed us and called us to a high calling in Christ Jesus. You have given us a place in the fellowship of Your Spirit and the witness of Your Church.

RESPONSE   We praise Your holy name, O Lord.

MINISTER   In darkness You have been our light, in adversity and temptation a rock of strength, in our joys the very spirit of joy, in our labors the all-sufficient reward.

RESPONSE   We praise Your holy name, O Lord.

MINISTER   You have remembered us when we have forgotten You, followed us even when we fled from You, met us with forgiveness when we turned back to You. For all Your longsuffering and the abundance of Your grace

RESPONSE   We praise Your holy name, O Lord.

The Offering

THE DOXOLOGY   (*all*)

The Meeting of Human Needs   (*At our tables we shall discuss various ways we can observe Lent, and help meet specific human needs that have been raised by members of our group.*)

Our Prayers of Dedication

PEOPLE LEFT   O Lord, we pray for the structures of government in our cities;

PEOPLE RIGHT   And for those who have no voice in them.

LEFT   We pray for families who are seeking their mission in life;

RIGHT   And for broken homes where parents or children live in fear, anger, or loneliness.

LEFT   We pray for world leaders and the United Nations as they seek to bring peace to a troubled world;

RIGHT   And for those who suffer from war's consequences.

LEFT   We pray for colleges and universities where the future is being created;

RIGHT   And for those who are frightened by where the truth leads them.

LEFT   We pray for those who have personal needs;

RIGHT   And for those who help to meet them.

LEFT   We pray for those who find new ways to love those around them;

RIGHT   And for those who are not able to love.

LEFT   We pray for those who reach out and seek God!

RIGHT   And for those who have not yet realized that He is seeking them.

LEFT   We pray for those who have decided to be in missions;

RIGHT   And for those who have not yet understood what it means to be the church.

LEFT   Our words must be followed by our deeds.

RIGHT   We assume responsibility for all for which we have prayed.

TOGETHER   Let us overcome all obstacles—and do it! Amen.

THE HYMN OF DEDICATION   "We Shall Overcome"

The Benediction

PALM SUNDAY SERVICE [6]

Theme: "The Last Week" *with Scripture readings throughout from The New English Bible.*

Sunday—The Triumphant Entry
NARRATOR *reads Mark 10:32–35.*

CHOIR   "On the Way to Jerusalem" (*During the singing,* CHILDREN *enter in procession down the aisles waving palm branches. They take their places in the front pews.*)

NARRATOR *reads Luke 19:38–44.*

SOLOIST   "The Holy City"

PRAYER FOR THE CHURCH (*in unison*)   Our Father, we meet in Your church—the fellowship which is Your body, and the instrument through which salvation is proclaimed. We thank You for our membership in it. We recall with gratitude Your Son who founded the church, and who gave Himself for it in the historically shattering acts of this week. The way in which His life ended in misery and was renewed in the glory of the Resurrection still fills us with great wonder.

We can worship You today, because You live with Your church forever. We can rejoice in the hope of a better world which You have made possible. Help us to exhibit that faith which builds a better future and a virile community dedicated to Jesus Christ, our Lord and Saviour, who taught His followers to pray, saying:

Our Father in heaven, holy be Your Name, Your kingdom come, Your will be done, on earth as in heaven. Give us today our daily bread. Forgive us our sins as we forgive those who sin against us. Do not bring us to the test, but deliver us from evil. For the kingdom, the power, and the glory are Yours now and forever. Amen.

Monday—The Cleansing of the Temple   *A drama, centered around the offertory, performed by the* USHERS *or* STEWARDS. *Use as many as are normally required to receive the offering. They come forward; two (if possible the* STEWARDSHIP CHAIRMAN *and the* TREASURER *of the church) stand facing the* CONGREGATION. *The others pick up or receive the offering plates, and stand facing the two leaders.*

STEWARDSHIP CHAIRMAN   I am the Stewardship Chairman of this church. Here is a list of the contributions required from our members. Please collect these dues. (*He holds up a list—any document will do!—and offers it to them.*)

FIRST STEWARD No one has the right to say how much any member must give to the Lord's work.

SECOND STEWARD Good stewardship means the effective use of everything we possess to glorify God.

THIRD STEWARD Every member has the responsibility to give to the church the first fruits of his labor, supporting God's work as the Lord has prospered him.

STEWARDSHIP CHAIRMAN The Bible calls for a tithe—10 percent of family income. Instruct the people to place their dues in the offering plates, according to this list based on family income.

FIRST STEWARD We will receive from the people what God prompts them in their hearts to give. Your list has no place in this church.

TREASURER I am the treasurer. In order to pay these bills (he waves a handful of papers in the air), we will require $1,827. That means $12.73 from every member. (*Adjust these figures to appear realistic in the local situation.*)

FOURTH STEWARD The debts of the church are never paid. Until the day when "every knee shall bow, and every tongue acknowledge God" (Romans 14:11), there will always be cost and sacrifice required for the church to be the body of Christ, preaching, teaching, ministering in His name.

FIFTH STEWARD On this day, Jesus drove the money changers out of the temple, saying, "My house shall be called a house of prayer, but you have made it a robbers' cave" (Matthew 21:13). Let us have no part in collecting dues, changing money, and paying bills in God's house. Paul, writing to the church at Corinth, declared:

STEWARDS (*turn and face the* CONGREGATION, *in unison*) "Each person should give as he has decided for himself; there should be no reluctance, no sense of compulsion; God loves a cheerful giver" (2 Corinthians 9:7).

(*The offering is then received, after which the* CONGREGATION *sings the hymn,* "We Give Thee But Thine Own." *During the last verse, the* STEWARDS *bring the offering forward. The* CONGRE-

GATION *remains standing, while the* MINISTER *offers a prayer of dedication.*)

Tuesday—Jesus Denounces the Religious Establishment (*Meditation by the* MINISTER, *about ten minutes, based on Jesus' teaching in Matthew 21:23–32. Conclude with the congregational hymn, "The Church's One Foundation." This may be sung with organ stop variations, descant, and/or instrumental accompaniment.*)

Wednesday—Teaching in the Temple (*A mimed drama based on Matthew 21:33–43. This section is acted in silence by the* CHILDREN *who come forward from the front pews as needed.*)

NARRATOR   Listen to another parable. There was a landowner who planted a vineyard. (CHILD *comes forward; goes through the actions of planting.*)

NARRATOR   . . . He put a wall around it, made a winepress, and built a watchtower, then he let it out to vinegrowers and went abroad. (*Other children as* BUILDERS *come forward, work in twos and threes in actions of building. Some go through the motions of constructing a high tower. Finally, they all stand back. The* LANDOWNER *gives them instructions in mimed speech and gestures and then departs, accompanied by several of the* BUILDERS.)

NARRATOR   When the vintage season approached, he sent his servants to the tenants to collect the produce due to him. (*Those who went out with the* LANDOWNER, *now return.*)
   But they took his servants, thrashed one, killed another and stoned a third. (*This is acted out.*)

NARRATOR   Again, he sent other servants, and they did the same to them. (*This is acted out. There are now bodies lying around everywhere.*)

NARRATOR   At last, he sent to them his son. "They will respect my son," he said. But when they saw the son, the tenants said to one another, "That is the heir. Come on, let us kill him and get his inheritance." And they took him, flung him out of the vineyard and killed him. (*The action continues.*)

NARRATOR When the owner of the vineyard comes, how do you think he will deal with those tenants? "He will bring those bad men to a bad end," they answer, "and hand the vineyard over to other tenants, who will let him have his share of the crop when the season comes." (*The* LANDOWNER *returns and drives the* TENANTS *away. The bodies remain on the floor. The* LANDOWNER *returns to the front pew.*)

NARRATOR Then Jesus said to them, "Can it be that you have never read this text, 'The stone which the builders rejected has become the main corner-stone. This is the Lord's doing and it is wonderful in our eyes.' Therefore, I tell you the Kingdom of God will be taken away from you and given to a nation that wants the proper fruit." (*The bodies can now sit up, but they should remain seated on the floor gathered around the* NARRATOR *or pulpit.*)

Thursday—Gethsemane

ANTHEM "Into the Woods My Master Went" (*words by Sidney Lanier*) (*Mimed drama based on Mark 14:32–50. This is acted out in a similar way to the parable on Wednesday. As the reading commences, a child representing* JESUS *enters. This can be the same child as the landowner in the previous section. He is accompanied by three* DISCIPLES *who can be the vine-growers from the previous section. He speaks to the* DISCIPLES *and leaves them with the other children to pray, while he moves to one corner, kneels down and assumes an attitude of prayer. The reading of Mark 14:32 begins and is interrupted at verse 36. Then the Pastoral Prayer follows.*)

LEADER Let us pray.

Most gracious God, when we pause to think of the future, both of our own lives and of this world, we are very uncertain. Is there suffering ahead for us? We turn to You today, seeking strength and reassurance.

PEOPLE Abba, Father, all things are possible to You; take this cup away from us. Yet, not what we desire, but what You require.

LEADER Sometimes we have sought self-fulfillment at the expense of other people. Sometimes we have been so caught up in the struggle to keep up with our neighbors, that we have discovered the hard way that he who saves his life loses it, and we have become panicky about the direction of our own lives, about our family, about our friends, about our nation, and about the millions in the world who suffer great hardships.

PEOPLE Abba, Father, all things are possible to You; take this cup away from us. Yet, not what we desire, but what You require.

LEADER We have neglected the things that belong to our peace, and pursued the things that belong to our pleasure and self-gratification. We know we should be seeking ways to turn the budgets of the nations away from bombs and bullets, away from suppression and enslavement toward the purchase of bread, the wine of communion with Christ, the mark of kindness that provides medicine and machinery to instruct the human community in justice and peace. Deep down, we know what we should be doing, but our inertia and fear of personal sacrifice prevents us from acting.

PEOPLE Abba, Father, all things are possible to You; take this cup away from us. Yet, not what we desire, but what You require.

LEADER Lord, pull our lives together in a living unity. Wake us up, and point us in the direction You want for Your disciples, that we might in word and deed proclaim the gospel of salvation to every creature.

PEOPLE Abba, Father, all things are possible to You; take this cup away from us. Yet, not what we desire, but what You require.

ALL Make us the kind of men and women who make things happen, who are the cause of growth in others, the witnesses by whom men everywhere may come to know Christ as Lord and Saviour, who can in Christ's Name make the lame walk, the blind see, and the deaf hear! Make us more eager to serve than to be served. In the Name of Jesus, our Lord and Master, we pray. Amen.

(*Reading continues at verse 37.* JESUS *returns, and finds all the* DISCIPLES *asleep. He awakens first* PETER, *then, by gestures, all of the* DISCIPLES, *expressing His disappointment by gesture through verses 39 and 40. He moves away again, though perhaps not returning to His former position, and the* DISCIPLES *go to sleep again. He returns and awakens the* DISCIPLES *a second and third time. At verse 42, all the* DISCIPLES *stand. At verse 43, more children, representing* JUDAS *and the crowd, enter. At verse 45,* JUDAS *kisses* JESUS *in the Jewish manner of cheek to cheek. The others seize him in a mild melee. At verse 48,* JESUS *stands on His dignity and remonstrates with them. At verse 50,* JESUS *is led out and the other* DISCIPLES *slip quickly away, back to their pews.*)

Friday—Trial and Crucifixion [7]

ANTHEM "March to Calvary"—Maunder (*Following the anthem sung by the* CHOIR, *the hymn responses may be sung or spoken.*)

CHOIR

> Ah Holy Jesus, how hast Thou offended
> That man to judge Thee hath in hate pretended?
> By foes derided, by Thine own rejected,
> O most afflicted!

CONGREGATION (*read in unison*)

> Who was the guilty? Who brought this upon Thee?
> Alas, my treason, Jesus, hath undone Thee!
> Twas I, Lord Jesus, I it was denied Thee:
> I crucified Thee.

CHOIR

> Were you there when they crucified my Lord?
> Were you there when they nailed Him to the tree?
> Oh, sometimes it causes me to tremble,
> Were you there when they crucified my Lord?

NARRATOR

> O come and mourn with me awhile;
> O come ye to the Saviour's side;
> O come, together let us mourn;
> Jesus, our Lord, is crucified!

SOLO

> Seven times He spake, seven words of love;
> And all three hours His silence cried
> For mercy on the souls of men:
> Jesus, our Lord, is crucified!

CHOIR

> O break, O break, hard heart of mine!
> Thy weak self-love and guilty pride
> His Pilate and His Judas were:
> Jesus, our Lord, is crucified!

ALL (*sing*)

> O love of God! O sin of man!
> In this dread act your strength is tried,
> And victory remains with love:
> Jesus, our Lord, is crucified!

NARRATOR

> O sacred Head, now wounded, With grief and shame
>   weighed down;
> Now scornfully surrounded With thorns, Thine
>   only crown;
> O sacred Head, what glory, What bliss till now
>   was Thine!
> Yet, though despised and gory, I joy to call
>   Thee mine.

CHOIR

> What language shall I borrow To thank Thee,
>   dearest Friend,
> For this Thy dying sorrow, Thy pity without end?
> O make me Thine forever; And should I fainting be,
> Lord, let me never, never Outlive my love to Thee.

CONGREGATION (*read in unison*)

> Behold the lamb of God, who takes away the
> sin of the world!

ANTHEM   "Behold The Lamb of God"—Matthew Bridges

NARRATOR

> Cross of Jesus, cross of sorrow,
> Where the blood of Christ was shed,

Perfect man on thee did suffer,
Perfect God on thee has bled!

ALL (*sing, remaining seated*) "Cross of Jesus, Cross of Sorrow"

CONGREGATION (*read in unison*) This Son of Man must be lifted up as the serpent was lifted up by Moses in the wilderness, so that everyone who believes in Him may in Him possess eternal life.

ANTHEM "God So Loved the World"—Stainer

CONGREGATION God so loved the world, that He gave His only begotten Son, that who so believeth in Him should not perish, but have everlasting life. For God sent not His Son into the world to condemn the world, but that the world through Him might be saved.

Saturday—Silence and Mourning (*Period of silent meditation, about 4 minutes. At the end of this time, the organ sounds chimes, and soft music in a minor key. The* USHERS *come forward and guide the* PEOPLE *to leave the sanctuary in silence. From the front pew to the rear, in order, the* PEOPLE *file out. The* USHERS *will guide everyone to a lounge or suitable area elsewhere in the building where there will be coffee and fellowship. Here the* GREETERS *and* MINISTER *will meet the* PEOPLE. *Note that the benediction is omitted.*)

UPPER ROOM SERVICE

For small group, or a setting for a twenty-four-hour prayer vigil either during the week before Easter or any other suitable time. Room is set with a communion table spread with twelve places. A communion tray of cups, a small loaf, a Bible and a lighted candle is at each place with a chair, or kneeler. A large pulpit Bible is opened to the Mark 14 account of the upper-room happening, and set in the center of the table with one large candle representing Christ. All candles are lighted: the twelve on the communion table and the large candle. Other lights are turned off or dimmed.

No actual service is led. Persons come for private meditation, prayer, and communion. If it is a prayer vigil, persons would come on the hour or half-hour to avoid disrupting worshipers.

Each person is directed to read the following Scriptures:

Matthew 26:17–30

Matthew 26:36–56

Suggested Prayer Thoughts:

PRAY THAT YOU MAY BE

> able to suffer without complaining,
> to be misunderstood without explaining;
> able to endure without a breaking,
> to be forsaken without forsaking;
> able to give without receiving,
> to be ignored without grieving;
> able to ask without commanding,
> to love despite misunderstanding;
> able to turn to the Lord for guarding,
> able to wait for His own rewarding!

(*Each may partake of the communion elements when he desires, and leave when he wishes.*)

EASTER FESTIVAL OF THE DAWN

Gathering Outdoor Music   (BAND, *a brass ensemble in front of sanctuary*)

Processional March "Christ, the Lord Is Risen Today"

(CHOIR *proceeds down center aisle, then moves to outside aisles with the* CONGREGATION *following behind led by a person with a banner. They march around the interior of the sanctuary or around the outside of the building; or, the entire* CONGREGATION *may be requested to gather in an adjacent building such as a gym, or in a parking area. When the music begins, the people follow in two lines behind the* BAND *ensemble and* CHOIR *as they process to sanctuary and worship. The organ joins in the march music as the procession enters the sanctuary. Several banners should be spaced and carried in the processional with such words as,* "He Is Risen!"; "Live!")

Litany "Healings from the Empty Tomb"

LEADER Men of God, why do you seek the living among the dead?

RESPONSE Because we are afraid, we are uncertain, we are uncomfortable here, and we have doubts about this Man.

LEADER Do not be afraid, for He has risen from the dead, He has broken through the tomb, He has come back to life and He is here among us now.

Men of God, why do you seek the living among the dead?

RESPONSE Because we feel guilty, we feel lonely, and we feel lost, for we deserted that Man.

LEADER Do not carry your guilt any longer, for He has taken the guilt Himself, He has buried it in His grave, He has lifted it to His cross, and He is here among us now.

Men of God, why do you seek the living among the dead?

RESPONSE Because our wounds are deep. We have torn away from that man, we have broken with Him and with our fellowmen.

LEADER Do not dwell on your wounds for He has risen to heal you, He has risen to forgive you, He has risen to change you all and bind us all together now.

Men of God, He is not here; He is risen.

RESPONSE Yes, He is risen!

LEADER   He is risen!
RESPONSE   And He is here!
LEADER   Allelu!
RESPONSE   Allelu!
LEADER   He is risen!
RESPONSE   And He is here! [8]

Unison Prayer   Heavenly Father, we tremble on the threshold of this day's wonder, lost for words. Like the disciples we have often felt Jesus' life was coming to nothing; then He startles us with a greeting and disturbs us with His presence. You have raised Him from the dust of death, and suddenly all life takes on a new perspective. Fill us now with the joy and excitement of believing, in Jesus Christ. Amen.

CHORAL RESPONSE   "Gloria Patri"

WITNESS FROM THE ANCIENT WORD   1 Corinthians 15:12–28

Reading from the Now

EASTER

Universe
and every universe beyond,
spin and blaze,
whirl and dance,
leap and laugh
as never before.
It's happened.
It's new.
It's here.
The liberation.
The victory.
The new creation.
Christ has smashed death.
He has liberated the world.
He has freed the universe.
You and I and everything
are free again,
new again,
alive again.

> Let's have a festival
> and follow Him across the skies,
> through the flames of heaven
> and back down every alley of our town.
> There, let's have Him come
> to liberate our city
> clean up the mess
> and start all over again.
> You conquered.
> Keep on fighting through us.
> You arose.
> Keep on rising in us.
> You celebrated.
> Keep on celebrating with us.
> You happen.
> You are new.
> You are here.[9]

Affirmation of Faith We confess that Jesus is the Christ, the Son of the living God, and proclaim Him Lord and Saviour of the world. In His name and by His grace we accept our mission of witness and service to mankind. We rejoice in God our Father, maker of heaven and earth, and in the covenant of love by which He has bound us to Himself. Through baptism into Christ we enter into newness of life and are made one with the whole people of God. In the fellowship and communion of the Holy Spirit we are joined to one another in brotherhood and in obedience to Christ. At the table of the Lord we celebrate with thanksgiving His saving acts and His presence. Within the universal church we receive the gift of ministry and the light of Scripture. In the bonds of Christian faith we yield ourselves to God, that we may serve Him whose kingdom has no end. Blessing, glory, and honor be to Him forever. Amen.[10]

ANTHEM "I Know That My Redeemer Liveth"

The Homily "From Sunset To Sunrise" Easter is a festival of the dawn! Clement of Alexandria, one of the early church fathers, caught the significance of Easter when he wrote: "Christ has turned our sunsets into sunrise." In the Resurrection narrative itself, the record says, "They came unto the sepulchre at the rising of the sun" (Mark 16:2 KJV) and life was never the same again.

At sunset, it seemed that the universe did not care what happened to its righteous; at sunrise, the disciples knew that at its heart was an Invincible Power, that it was designed by benevolent intelligence, tempered by limitless love, directed by holy purpose.

At sunset, the cross seemed a horrible implement of execution from which everyone cringed; at sunrise, it became a reverent and holy symbol, before which the world kneels in adoration and rises with inspiration.

At sunset, the grave, sealed with an immovable boulder and heavily guarded, seemed conclusive evidence that death was the end; with the coming of dawn, however, was the proof that man has forever, and outlives death; the grave represents an expectant adventure into life eternal. "O death, where is thy sting? O grave, where is thy victory?"

At sunset, only minor chords of hopeless existence were heard; at sunrise, the exhuberant harmonies of joyous and meaningful living were sung.

At sunset, a Galilean rabbi, Jesus of Nazareth, was dead; at sunrise, He was truly the Christ of God, the risen Lord of Glory.

At sunset, the obscure disciples were a timid, discouraged, disillusioned, weary lot; at sunrise, they were transformed, confident, courageous crusaders who went forth to defy kings, to proclaim Christ, and to change the world.

Easter was the day that changed the world. Easter is the festival of the dawn. If you can catch the spirit, power, and significance of this day, it can turn your sunsets into sunrises.

The Easter dawn should turn your questions into renewed certainty of life's invisibles. Thomas, the hard-headed logician, was the typical materialist among the disciples. His faith, like the others, had dwindled completely when Jesus died. When it was announced that Jesus had risen and was alive, he replied, "Except I see, I will not believe." Then the risen Lord appeared, and Thomas, falling down, cried, "My Lord, my God." Jesus said, "Because you have seen me, you believe; blessed are they who have not seen me but who believe."

". . . he hath given assurance unto all men, in that he hath raised him from the dead" (Acts 17:31 KJV).[11]

DEDICATION HYMN   "Look Ye Saints! The Sight Is Glorious"

The Offering

STEWARDSHIP SENTENCE   "Ascribe to the Lord the glory due his name; bring an offering, and come into his courts . . ." (Psalm 96:8).

SONG   "Allelu"

The Resurrection Community Feast—The Eucharist Good News

LEADER   We declare ourselves to be the Easter community.

PEOPLE   We are here because Jesus is the good news for all people.

LEADER   He took the sad news of our sin and guilt and turned it around through His dying for it and rising for us.

PEOPLE   Now, we are a part of that new people in Christ, and come here to celebrate His Resurrection and presence.

LEADER   Jesus was broken for us and torn apart for us to be healed.

PEOPLE   He rose from the grave to unleash new life in the world.

LEADER   He took the bread, blessed it, and broke it. He said to His friends, "Take, eat; this is my body."

PEOPLE   So He took a cup, filled with fruit of the vine. After thanks, He gave it to them saying, "Drink of it, all of you; for this is my blood of the covenant."

LEADER   "[It] is poured out for many for the forgiveness of sins."

PRAYER OF THANKSGIVING   O Living Master, take us as unworthy as we are, into the fellowship of Your redeemed. We acknowledge our shortcomings and our sins, our inconsistent minds and hearts, and our slackness of devotion. But You do not forsake us even when we betray You. So accept us not for what

we are, but for what You can create in us. We thank You that
our individual lives can be more complete as we live in communion with You, O Christ, and with others. In Your Spirit.
Amen.

Partaking (*As each member passes the bread to his neighbor,
he says,* "Feeding you in His name, I give you bread.")

(*As each member passes the cup to his neighbor, he says,*
"Feeding you in His name, I give you the cup.")

The Kiss of Peace
ANTHEM   "The Hallelujah Chorus"—Handel

EASTERTIDE FESTIVAL—(THE RESURRECTION
OF A COMMUNITY) [12]

The Silent Processional

The Call to Worship
LEADER   Good Morning! Easter is past. Why are you people here?
PEOPLE   It is the season of Eastertide and we have come to
celebrate the Resurrection.
LEADER   The Resurrection of our Lord Jesus Christ?
PEOPLE   Yes. And the resurrection of the community of believers.
LEADER   God raised Him and He raised us as witnesses.
PEOPLE   And we are gathered here to thank Him, praise Him
and respond to Him.
LEADER   In His Name and for His sake,
PEOPLE   Amen.
THE HYMN (*standing*)   "Shout for Joy"

The Confession and Thanksgiving (*standing*)
LEADER   In the midst of flashing neon darkness,

PEOPLE   We thank You God for light.
LEADER   In the midst of blaring, shouting silence,
PEOPLE   We thank You God for the Word.
LEADER   In the midst of bloated, gorged starvation,
PEOPLE   We thank you God for bread.
LEADER   In the midst of bottled, bubbling thirst,
PEOPLE   We thank You God for water.
LEADER   In the midst of smothered, gnawing doubt,
PEOPLE   We thank You God for an affirmation.
LEADER   In the midst of frantic, laughing death,
PEOPLE   We thank You God for life.
LEADER   Sing alleluia—rejoice! . . . with trembling.
THE HYMN (*standing*)   "Lord of the Dance"

The Silent Meditation

The Pastoral Prayer   Heavenly Father, We hear the news that Jesus is raised from the corruption of death, and walks this creation as the Prince of Glory. We pray for this tired old world with its drugged illusions, that it may awaken to the new morning, and shine in Your splendid light.

We pray for men and women who have compromised with evil, and find themselves on a downward path into the frightening dark.

We pray for those who have achieved the security they sought, but find themselves disappointed with only a semblance of life.

We pray for men and women who receive life with all its promise, and succeed only in burying it in the ground.

Please make us understand that as You raised Jesus from the dead You can recreate us to live in true glory.

Through Jesus Christ our Lord.[12a]

The Lord's Prayer

The Word
LEADER   We praise God,
PEOPLE   For His gifts of life, of love, of freedom, of hope!

LEADER Let us listen now to the Drama of Creation. (*The drama of creation as found in Genesis 1:26–31, and followed by the congregation's response.*)

LEADER God of Creation.

PEOPLE We thank You for your gift of LIFE!

LEADER Let us listen now to the Drama of Incarnation. (*The drama of incarnation as found in John 1:9–15, and followed by the congregation's response.*)

LEADER God Incarnate,

PEOPLE We thank You for Your gift of LOVE shown to us by Jesus Christ!

LEADER Let us listen now to the Drama of Redemption. (*The drama of redemption as found in John 3:14–18, followed by the congregation's response.*)

LEADER God of Redemption,

PEOPLE We thank You for Your gift of FREEDOM made possible by the death of Jesus Christ!

LEADER Let us listen now to the Drama of Salvation. (*The drama of salvation as found in John 20:30, 31 and Acts 2:42–47, followed by the congregation's response.*)

LEADER God of Salvation,

PEOPLE We thank You for Your gift of HOPE illustrated by the RESURRECTION!

LEADER God we thank You

PEOPLE for LIFE,

LEADER for LOVE,

PEOPLE for FREEDOM,

LEADER for HOPE!

PEOPLE Amen!

THE HYMN "They'll Know We Are Christians by Our Love"

The Affirmation of Faith (*standing*)

LEADER Christian! In what do you believe?

PEOPLE I believe in God, who created me.

LEADER And, what else?

PEOPLE I believe in Jesus Christ, who died to set me free.

LEADER And, what else?

PEOPLE I believe in the Holy Spirit, the presence of God I experience in my life.

LEADER And, what else?

PEOPLE I believe I am part of a community that has been resurrected to witness to His action and respond to His love.

LEADER And, what else?

PEOPLE I believe that I respond to God's love by loving others and that the Kingdom of God will come upon the earth.

LEADER Let us live our belief!

THE GLORIA PATRI (*standing*)

THE OFFERING HYMN "Lord, I Want To Be a Christian." (*During the singing of this hymn, individuals may take their gifts to the altar for dedication. The hymn will be sung through as many times as necessary to allow all who wish to take their offering forward.*)

The Celebration of The Resurrected Community (*When the* LITURGIST *comes down, the entire* CONGREGATION *will join into one physical unit, back and forth across aisles and pews, with each worshiper holding the hands of two others. The* CONGREGATION *will remain this way through the silent prayer, hymn, and benediction.*)

THE HYMN (*standing, united*) "Blest Be the Tie That Binds" (*one verse*)

THE BENEDICTION (*standing, united*) We have met Jesus of Nazareth, and for that reason the concerns of the whole world are our concerns. In the prayers of this community, we go now from this place with the intention to live for others. The Lord be with you. Go. Serve in His Name.

The Passing of the Peace (*After the benediction, the peace will be passed by each person to nearby worshipers by clasping both hands and passing the greeting, "Peace to you!"*)

FAMILY COMMUNION SERVICE

The dining room is the center of our homes—where the family congregates to eat—at least for special occasions. The family meal helps constitute the family as much as anything in contemporary society; it suggests togetherness. Guests may be invited to share the evening. Banners, pictures, posters or other visual arts suggesting the Lord and His gifts may be placed in the room. Flowers may be scattered on the table as a sign of joy and beauty.

The meal begins by the family singing:

> For health and strength
> and daily food
> We praise Thy name.
> O Lord.

(*Following, the family members hold hands, forming a circle, while the grace prayer is given*) "We thank You, God, for Your faithful love and kind providence to our family. Bless this food to our health and the worship to Your glory and our spiritual strength. In Jesus' name. Amen." (*During the meal, a jovial atmosphere is desired, with conversation centered on the happy experiences, and the goodness of the Lord.*)

The Communion Service   (*A loaf of unsliced bread and a single chalice of grape juice are brought to the leader's plate along with an open Bible. After the meal, the lights are dimmed, candles lighted.*)

HEAD OF TABLE   As this meal has unified us together as a family, just so the Lord's Supper helps to build us up into the family of God. Since the first century, the Lord's Supper has been a stylized meal with bread and wine.

HOSTESS Let us hear the words of Scripture: "When we ask the Lord's blessing upon our drinking from the cup of wine at the Lord's Table, this means, doesn't it, that all who drink it are sharing together the blessing of Christ's blood? And when we break off pieces of the bread from the loaf to eat there together, this shows that we are sharing together in the benefits of his body. No matter how many of us there are, we all eat from the same loaf, showing that we are all parts of the one body of Christ" (1 Corinthians 10:16, 17 LB).

SONG "Sons of God"

The Liturgy of the Loaf

HEAD OF TABLE The Lord's Supper is the sacrament of unity in Christ. In Christ we become close to one another. Let it be known to all that Christ is the head of this family, that He is Lord of this home. Let us pray:

ALL (*have this prayer on a card at each place at the table*) O Lord, may each one of us, and all of us together be aware just now of the Divine Presence which is here with us. As we celebrate with great joy the coming of the Christ, may we ever remember His presence here now with all of us who gather in His Name. Amen.

ONE OF THE CHILDREN These words came from John concerning the coming of Christ, "In the beginning was the Word, and the Word was with God, and the Word was God . . . And the Word became flesh and dwelt among us, full of grace and truth" (John 1:1, 14).

SECOND CHILD These words come to us from Jesus Himself, "I am come that [you] may have life and have it more abundantly" (John 10:10).

THIRD CHILD (*or the second if only two*) These are our Lord's words to Nicodemus, "For God so loved the world that he gave his only Son that whoever believes in him should not perish but have eternal life. For God sent his Son into the world, not to condemn the world, but that the world might be saved through him" (John 3:16, 17).

HEAD OF TABLE   As we break the loaf and share the bread with
  each other, let us feel a kinship with each other, and with all
  the others of our spiritual family who join with us. May the
  physical and spiritual strength that we have gained here bind
  us more closely together. May it send us forth with more vigor
  and enthusiasm, in order that we may be better servants of
  our Lord. Let us pray:
ALL (*on prayer card*)   O Lord, accept our thanks for this loaf
  and all that it means to us: for the sense of family; for the
  sense of family within the church; for the understanding of
  our servant role and the need for the strengthening of the
  servants; for an awareness of the Divine Presence in all phases
  of our living. In the Name of our Lord Jesus Christ we pray.
  Amen.

Partaking of Communion Emblems   (*Without any words, all
follow the lead of the* HEAD OF THE TABLE. *He passes the loaf,
each tears from it and eats. Then he passes the chalice. Each
drinks from it as it passes. When everyone has finished, the*
HEAD "Passes the Peace" *concluding the service.*)

ECUMENICAL OR CONVENTION COMMUNION
SERVICE
Theme: "Unity In God's Family"

General Description   Service may be held in a large park, garden,
an indoor arena, or any area where chairs are movable. Place a
communion table crossing the center of the room from one side to
the other side. Going out from this table on both sides set rows of
twenty-five chairs each, facing one another. (The intention is to
develop the spirit of togetherness and oneness. Though all will not

be able to see all of the speakers, nevertheless they will be able to hear, and to become involved through the marching, singing, distributing, and partaking.) The platform for the speakers can be a raised portion in the midst of the communion table.

The delegates may be kept out of the room or garden until the processional. While they arrive in the gathering courtyard, a band (five saxophones, two trumpets, one trombone, one piano, one sousaphone, and a drummer) plays a thirty-minute prelude medley of religious music. When the time for entrance arrives, the worshipers will form a double line and march, singing celebration songs such as "Let's Celebrate, God Is Here," "Forward Through the Ages," "We're Marching to Zion" with the band leading.

In the procession banners are carried with such slogans as, ONE IN CHRIST; LOVE; GOD'S FAMILY, to be placed in the communion table area. Placards are also carried in the procession, with the denominations, states, or countries represented. They should be placed evenly throughout the gathering area. The processional might be more of a celebration if it were longer, taking the worshipers a distance, such as around the outer arena hall, or around the building before entering the communion hall or garden.

Persons are to be seated facing one another in areas with two rows of twenty-five chairs. One server is assigned each fifty people. One tray of cups and one loaf should be placed on the long communion table for each group of fifty. When the congregation is called upon to march and sing during the service, the area group of fifty marches in the elongated circle, shaking hands with those across as they march.

When serving, the deacon serves the first person seated the bread; he in turn gets up and serves the person across from him—so on down the two rows. After all have partaken of the loaf, the cup is served in like manner.

At the conclusion, the "peace" is passed from person to person, with the double handclasp and the words, "May the love of Christ keep us in peace"—and the response, "So may it ever be."

If possible, a luncheon or dinner (agape feast) might follow immediately in an adjacent area to further the fellowship ties.

(The program for the Ecumenical or Convention Communion Service follows. Refer to this general description for help in planning.)

Gathering Music Band (*see description*)

PROCESSIONAL MEDLEY "We're Marching to Zion," "Forward Through the Ages" (*When a seating area is complete, the smaller groups will march around the chairs.*)

Call to Celebration

LEADER Celebration is the mood of today's service. Cry out for joy for what God has done in Christ!

PEOPLE Amen! Amen! Amen!

LEADER "You are a chosen people. God's own people. Once you were no people but now you are God's people. Once you had not received mercy, but now you have received mercy" (1 Peter 2:9, 10). Clap your hands for joy!

PEOPLE (*clap their hands*)

LEADER Let us pray:

Father of the new humanity in Christ, we humble ourselves in thankfulness, for the knowledge of Your presence and salvation. Grant that we might worship You with genuine hearts, and adequately prepare to partake of the family meal.

PEOPLE We seek Your presence, Holy Father.

LEADER Let our love for each other become genuine and strong; let us know that where there is love, You are present also.

PEOPLE We seek to experience Your love, Loving Father.

LEADER Grant that Your love might enliven all of our relationships, so that we may know that Your church is present here.

PEOPLE We seek to be Your church, Forgiving Father, in Jesus' Name. Amen.

CHORAL RESPONSE "Gloria Patri"—Floyd E. Werle

CELEBRATING AS GOD'S FAMILY

INTERPRETER ONE "The Family of God"
(*This is a five-minute devotional thought based on communion as God's Family Feast using as the Scripture basis Ephesians 2:19 and 1 Peter 2:9, 10.*)

HYMN "In Christ There Is No East or West"

(*As this hymn is sung, persons in group-arranged chairs will march in circle, shaking hands with those in their circle; even talking a bit if music continues after singing is concluded.*)

PRAYER OF THANKSGIVING (*standing; may raise arms if wish*)
To be accepted into Your family, O God, is great! To be a part of this historic people, O God, is wonderful! To be called to a mission of love is exciting. We come asking for nothing but a thankful spirit, in Jesus' Name. Amen.

CONFESSING OUR BROKENNESS

INTERPRETER TWO   "The Shameful Divisions in the Family"
(*This is a five-minute devotional thought based on God's Family, now divided, and Christ's will that the church be one. The Scripture basis for this devotional is John 17:9–23.*)

UNISON CONFESSION PRAYER (WORSHIPERS *kneel at chair, or as seated, bowed in head, to gesture remorse by beating chest.*)
Let us pray: O God, we regret the splintered condition of Your church. How can the world become community, when we can't even be? We fullheartedly admit that we have done and said many wrong things that have hurt the church. We admit that we have neglected many opportunities to do loving things. Now we would turn away from these sins. Father, be merciful to us. Please forgive us. Turn us from our foolish ways, fill us with love and a desire to serve Thee all of our days. In Jesus' Name. Amen.

HYMN   "Dear Lord and Father of Mankind"; or "Forgive" (*standing*)

ASSURANCE OF PARDON   Hear the Good News: If one is in Christ he becomes a new person altogether. The past is finished and gone. Everything is fresh and new. "Now you are no longer strangers to God and foreigners to heaven, but you are members of God's very own family, citizens of God's country, and you belong in God's household with every other Christian" (Ephesians 2:19 LB).

GESTURE OF RECONCILIATION   (*Persons across from each other embrace, head over one shoulder and then the other, whispering,* "God forgives you.")

CELEBRATING GROWING UNITY

INTERPRETER THREE   "The Walls Are Crumbling"
(*This is a five-minute devotional thought that the barriers between us are now being transcended and the walls are breaking down. Give examples of this around the world pointing out that this was our forefathers' dream and Jesus' prayer. The Scripture basis for this devotional is Ephesians 2:13–22, 4:1–6.*)
HYMN   "They'll Know We Are Christians by Our Love"

Offering To Express Fraternal Love

Litany On Church Unity [13]

LEADER   And Jesus said, "Thou art Peter, and upon this rock I will build my church."

RESPONSE   "And the gates of hell will not prevail against it."

LEADER   Because I love little country churches, hid among elms and birches; crying babes in arms, preachers unalarmed.

RESPONSE   I love Thy kingdom, Lord, the house of Thine abode.

LEADER   I love city churches—inner-city churches, pointing ever to past accomplishments; yearning, hoping for a better day.

RESPONSE   The church our blest Redeemer saved with His own precious blood.

LEADER   I love black churches, with solid preaching, rousing music, handclapping; endless rounds of Amens and Hallelujahs.

RESPONSE   I love Thy Church, O God! Her walls before Thee stand.

LEADER   I love Catholic churches—stately spires with traditional crosses pointing heavenward; odors of incense and candles burning.

RESPONSE   Dear as the apple of Thine eye, and graven on Thy hand.

LEADER   I love mission churches in mushrooming new areas at home or deep in the bowels of Africa, Asia—telling of Christ, often making little headway.

RESPONSE For her my tears shall fall, for her my prayers ascend.

LEADER I love house churches—people seated on carpeted floors, coffee cups rattling; with the sincere seeking and searching out new ways.

RESPONSE To her my cares and toils be given, till toils and cares shall end.

LEADER I love Quaker churches—a respite from much talking with periods of deep meditation; and occasional head-nodding; Holy Spirit moving.

RESPONSE Beyond my highest joy, I praise her heavenly ways.

LEADER I love denominational churches—members often confused as to ownership. Is it Chloe, Paul, Apollos, Cephas; Luther, Calvin, Christ?

RESPONSE Her sweet communion, solemn vows, her hymns of love and praise.

LEADER I love institutional churches, now under attack; assembling baskets for the needy, tending wedding receptions; preaching Christ.

RESPONSE Jesus, Thou Friend divine, our Saviour and our King!

LEADER I love problem churches—old as the New Testament and as new as the last church council meeting, seeking improvement but often failing.

RESPONSE Thy hand from every snare and foe shall great deliv'rance bring.

LEADER I love Protestant suburban churches, somewhat sophisticated; well-organized; services and activities programmed to meet every need.

RESPONSE Sure as Thy truth shall last, to Zion shall be given—

LEADER I love all churches with endless "hypocrites" included and all manner of faults, mistakes; yet, ever heeding Christ in attempted mission.

RESPONSE The brightest glories earth can yield, and brighter bliss of heaven.

LEADER   "And all that believed were together, and had all things in common."

RESPONSE   And the Lord added to the Church—the country church, the city church, the black church, the Catholic church, the mission church, the house church, the Quaker church, the denominational church, the institutional church, the problem church, the suburban church, all churches—those that were being saved!

REALIZING OUR ONENESS

INTERPRETER FOUR   "One In Christ"
(This five-minute devotional thought is on the unifying power of Christ, the Head of the Church. This unity is realized in the communion of the Lord's Supper. The Scripture basis for this devotional is Colossians 1:13–20.)
HYMN   "Sons of God"
WORDS OF INSTITUTION:

> I hold in my hands a loaf of bread.
> I look at it . . . and see the fellowship of man.
> . . . for throughout the ages, the eating of bread
> together says, "We are one body. No one here is
> stranger or alien."
>
> I look at this bread . . . and see in it the
> common life in which we are fulfilled
> . . . for the labor of many makes it
> available to the one.
> In this bread I see human dignity
> . . . work is the gift of oneself to the
> whole of which one is part.
>
> I see in it the invisible life which sustains
> all people
> . . . no one can keep on being, apart
> from life's ever renewing.

> I look at this bread . . . and sense a wonder and
> mystery
> . . . for to nourish man is not the same as to
> fatten cattle. Food eaten by man is changed
> into the laughter and love of a person.[14]
> So we are at the beginning of a miracle
> . . . this bread becomes personal life;
> becomes the deeds of a people.

This cup is the new agreement between God and you that has been established and set in motion by Christ's love.

PARTAKE (*Each one serves the one across the loaf of bread. Then the cup.*)

WORDS OF ASSURANCE (*when communion is finished*) Isn't it heavenly? This is a foretaste of the Heavenly Kingdom—a world without end.

UNISON LORD'S PRAYER (*paraphrased*) Our Father, may all men come to respect and to love You. May You rule in every person and in all of life. Give us, day by day, the things of life we need. Forgive us our sins, for we forgive everyone who has done us wrong. Let nothing test us beyond our strength. Save us from our weakness. For Yours is the authority, and the power and the glory, forever. Amen.

PASSING OF THE PEACE (*started by each section* LEADER) "Brother _____ or Sister _____, may the love and peace of God be with you." RESPONSE "And with you."

HYMN "Blest Be the Tie That Binds"

AGAPE FEAST—DINNER FOR ALL

AGAPE FEAST AND EUCHARIST [15]

Agape Meal *This may be a regular Family Night Dinner of congregation, or may be a meal of food as in ancient days, such as herbs, nuts, hard rolls, roast lamb, olives, figs, beans, grapes, cucumbers, wild honey, pomegranates, and milk or grape juice.*

Introduction

LEADER   The Sacrament of the Holy Communion was practiced when the early Christians gathered and shared a common meal, much as we have done here tonight. It was a distinctive mark of their coming together. After the meal was over they would then take the common elements of bread and wine, bless them, and then all the persons present would share in the sacred Eucharist, "in remembrance of Jesus." As we have fellowshiped about these tables, let us now join in this Lord's Supper by uniting in this "Recollection of Jesus."

A Recollection of Jesus

LEADER   Let us remember Jesus:

Who, though He was rich, yet for our sakes became poor and dwelt among us.

Who was content to be subject to His parents, the child of a poor man's home.

Who lived for nearly thirty years the common life, earning His living with His own hands and declining no humble tasks.

Whom the common people heard gladly, for He understood their ways.

PEOPLE   Let this mind be in us which was in Jesus Christ.

LEADER   Let us remember Jesus:

Who was mighty in deed, healing the sick and disordered, using for others the powers He would not invoke for Himself.

Who refused to force men's allegiance.

Who was Master and Lord to His disciples, yet was among them as their companion and as one who served.

Whose meat was to do the will of the Father who sent Him.

PEOPLE   Let this mind be in us which was in Jesus Christ.

LEADER   Let us remember Jesus:

Who loved men, yet retired from them to pray, watched through the night, stayed in the wilderness, went up into a mountain, sought a garden.

Who, when He would help a tempted disciple, prayed for him.

Who prayed for the forgiveness of those who rejected Him, and for the perfecting of those who received Him.

Who observed good customs, but defied conventions which did not serve the purposes of God.

Who hated sin because He knew the cost of pride and selfishness, of cruelty and impurity to man, and still more to His Father in heaven.

PEOPLE   Let this mind be in us which was in Jesus Christ.

LEADER   Let us remember Jesus:

Who believed in men to the last and never despaired of them.

Who through all disappointment never lost heart.

Who disregarded His own comfort and convenience, and thought first of others' needs, and though He suffered long, was always kind.

Who, when He was reviled, reviled not again, and when He suffered, threatened not.

Who humbled Himself and carried obedience to the point of death, even death on the cross, wherefore God has highly exalted Him.

PEOPLE   May this mind be in us which was in Jesus Christ. O Christ, our only Saviour, so come to dwell in us that we may go forth with the light of Thy hope in our eyes, and with Thy faith and love in our hearts. Amen.

THE FILMSTRIP   "Listen, Christian!" [16]

THE ANTHEM   "The Baker Woman"

The baker woman in her humble lodge received the grain of wheat
from God.

For nine whole months the grain she stored, behold the handmaid
of the Lord.

Chorus:
Make us the bread, Mary, bake us the bread, we need to be fed.

The baker woman took the road which led to Bethlehem, the
House of Bread,

To knead the bread she labored thru the night and brought it
forth about midnight.

(*Chorus*)

She baked the bread for thirty years by the fire of her love and
the salt of her tears,

By the warmth of a heart so tender and bright, and the bread
was golden brown and white.

(*Chorus*)

After thirty years the bread was done, it was taken to town by
her only son,

The soft white bread to be given free, to the hungry people of
Galilee.

(*Chorus*)

For thirty coins the bread was sold, and a thousand teeth, so cold,
so cold,

Tore it to pieces on a Friday noon when the sun turned black
and red the moon.

(*Chorus*)

And when she saw the bread so white, the living bread she made
in a night,

Devoured as wolves devour our sheep, the baker woman began
to weep.

(*Chorus*)

But the baker woman's only son appeared to his friends when
three days had gone.
On the road we stood and they all said and they knew he did
the breaking of bread.
Lift up your head, Mary, for now we've been fed!

The Invitation

MINISTER Friends, if you sincerely want to turn your backs on
your sins, if you wish to be transformed from a patronizing
activist to an involved disciple, and desire to lead a new life
of love and compassion, then get ready to come to God in
faith, and, confident of His forgiveness, let us join in this
prayer of confession:

The Prayer of Confession

CONGREGATION O God, whom Jesus called "Father," we acknowledge in our efforts to be good, we have often done wrong.
We have been quick to say to one in distress, "Be of good
cheer," when what he really needed was a warm meal or a
new pair of shoes. We have served on committees and councils
which sought to be helpful to persons, but we really never
saw nor knew those we tried to help. We have discussed
poverty, injustice, and the problem of drugs, thinking that in
discussion we have fulfilled our responsibilities. We have
placed limits on our charity and so have eliminated certain
people from our concern. Forgive us. Please forgive us now.
And grant that our love for our fellow men will not be merely
in theory or words, but in sincerity and in practice. Amen.

The Words of Assurance

MINISTER God, our Father, has promised to forgive all who
sincerely turn to Him in faith. Even now He forgives us, and
sets us free. Henceforth live! Live not in fear but in His power
and love, knowing that nothing can separate us from His love.
Therefore, let us always rejoice in the Lord!

The Presentation of the Holy Sacrament

MINISTER (*holding one large loaf and one chalice*) "And as they were eating, he took bread, and blessed, and broke it, and gave it to them, and said, 'Take; this is my body.' And he took a cup, and when he had given thanks he gave it to them, and they all drank of it. And he said to them, 'This is my blood of the covenant, which is poured out for many'" (Mark 14:22–24).

THE SERVING OF THE SACRAMENT   (*Each person tears a piece of bread from the loaf, then dips it into the chalice as it is passed. All is silent during this rite.*)

The Prayer of Thanksgiving

LEADER   Let us give our lives to God!

PEOPLE   We do offer our lives to God!

LEADER   Together, let us give thanks to the Lord!

PEOPLE   For it is the least that we can do!

UNISON   O God, we thank You for this chance to begin again. We thank You for our brothers and find in them a reason for loving, a reason for living. Here and now we offer ourselves unto You. We are Yours, body and soul. Fill us with Your grace and goodness, and lead us to a new life together. For Your Name's sake. Amen.

The Hymn of Commitment—"Go Tell Everyone"

The Blessing

MINISTER   The service is ended. But our life in Jesus Christ goes on. We go now, in His Name, into all the world. Let your light so shine, and your joy be so obvious, that all who see you will come to praise God! Amen.

Section 4

WEDDING
CELEBRATIONS

Section 4

WEDDING
CELEBRATIONS

SMALL WEDDING IN CHAPEL [1]

The BRIDE *and* GROOM *greet their* GUESTS *at the door, giving to each the mimeographed order, "A Celebration of Life and Love."* GUESTS *will be seated for the beginning of the service. The* PARENTS *will all be seated together. The* CONGREGATION *will join in singing the hymns. During the second hymn the* BRIDE *and* GROOM *will enter the chancel area from opposite sides. There are no attendants and no processional otherwise. The greetings and marriage relationship are given by the* BRIDE *and* GROOM *facing the congregation; the covenant and ring exchange are given by the* BRIDE *and* GROOM *facing each other. At the beginning of the covenant of marriage, the two sets of* PARENTS *stand beside the* BRIDE *and* GROOM. *The* GUESTS *then form a circle around the* BRIDE, GROOM, PARENTS *and* MINISTER. *When the* PARENTS *finish their covenant, they join in the circle. For the eucharist sharing, the* COUPLE *is served first by the* MINISTER *at the prie-dieu, then the trays are passed around the circle for all to share. Following the benediction, the* BRIDE *and* GROOM *take two baskets of flowers from the chancel and give each person a flower, expressing a personal word of appreciation and peace.*

124

A CELEBRATION OF LIFE AND LOVE

CALL TO WORSHIP   Psalm 100

HYMN OF PRAISE   "Praise to the Lord" or "Thine Is the Glory"

Opening Sentences

LEADER   This is the message that you have heard from the beginning: that we should love one another.

PEOPLE   Then let us love one another for love is from God and is of the nature of life, and he who has loved has known God.

LEADER   In the beginning God said, "It isn't good for man to be alone, I will make a companion for him" (LB).

PEOPLE   Therefore shall be heard this day the voice of gladness and of mirth, the voice of the bridegroom and the voice of the bride; the voices of those who sing and the joy of those who join in the celebration with joy and thanksgiving.

HYMN OF FAITH   "Love Divine, All Love Excelling" or "All Creatures of Our God and King"

Greeting

MINISTER   Dear friends, this gathering is a time of joy and gladness. You have been asked to share in the marriage of _____ and _____. It signifies to them a stage in the process of becoming, of self-realization, for each of them and now for both together, one that began at an earlier time and will continue as each of them grows and their friendship deepens. It is for them a covenant of becoming and a continuing celebration of God's gift of love and life. Because they believe this, _____ and _____ are glad you are here to share in the joy of the celebration.

Statement of Faith (*1 John 1:1–7 by the* MINISTER)

Marriage Relationship

BRIDE   Love is a growing thing . . .

GROOM   . . . a growing awareness of the meaning of "otherness." Another self who stands outside your self, whose life is a mystery and a challenge, a vexation and a thing of wonder.

BRIDE   It comes from involvement and grows in living with a person, sharing with him, and building something with him. It requires energy and imagination.

GROOM   It is impossible for superiors and inferiors to love, since the superior can only condescend and the inferior only admire. Love means recognition between two equals, not exploiting each other's strengths or weaknesses, but rejoicing in each other's presence.

BRIDE   Love must be a band and yet not binding, else our freedom is stifled in the name of love, and with our freedom, our humanity is lost.

GROOM   It is a relationship of greater possibility and greater risk, for the power to create is the power to destroy.

BRIDE   Marriage then is not a bond made of words or promises or the clauses of a contract.

GROOM   For no set of rules or promises can possibly exhaust the demands love may come to make of you.

BRIDE   It is a special spirit or style of life between two people. And if it is there, no possible words will make it more sacred or worthwhile.

GROOM   If it is not, no special phrases will make it exist. The words are an affirmation of that spirit, not a substitute for it.

BRIDE   Marriage is an affirmation of the possibility and power of forgiveness.

GROOM   It must have permanence. It should be something to depend on, a rock to anchor against the storm, a place to come home to.

BRIDE   Yet its permanence is not that of a wall which shuts things out or seals something in. It should be free and open to the winds of God.

GROOM   It is a stage on the road of friendship and love and discovery.

BRIDE   It means opening yourself a little more to the possibilities of another self and life itself.

GROOM   Finally, it was meant to be a continuing celebration of the gift of life and love. For it is in sharing and joy that it is fulfilled.

Covenant of Marriage

PARENTS' COVENANT   We now reaffirm our continuing love for our child, and we recognize that henceforth our primary responsibility is not to one or the other, but to both of them together.

COVENANT OF BRIDE AND GROOM   Because of you, when I laugh I am free to laugh all my laughter. Because you are here, when I cry I can cry all my tears. We have little to offer one another but our vulnerabilities, but these we can offer. We will fill one another's cup but not drink from one. We will join our hands in search of the important things of life, growing in freedom and sharing in our mutual discoveries. May the love which prompted us to struggle toward this point be marked with reverence for each other and for life.

Seal of the Covenant

EXCHANGE OF RINGS   I give you this ring as a sign of our covenant, of my love, and that which is between us, a sign that now each of us is two.

COVENANT PRAYER (*given by* MINISTER)   Bless, O Lord, the covenant made by these two, in the Name of the Father, Son, and Holy Spirit. Amen.

MINISTER'S PRONOUNCEMENT   Since you _____ and you _____ have consented together to be married, and have witnessed the same before God and this group of your family and friends, and have committed love and faith in each other, and have sealed the covenant with rings, I announce that God has made you husband and wife.

OFFERTORY   "Jesu, Joy of Man's Desiring"

Eucharist (*see Introduction*)
SONG OF JOY   "Now Thank We All Our God"

Benediction

Passing of the Peace

CONTEMPORARY SANCTUARY WEDDING [2]

The Organ Recital

Rejoice Greatly, O My Soul	Karg-Elert
Jesu, Joy of Man's Desiring	Bach-Grace
Basse et Dessus de Trompette	Cherambault
From God I Ne'er Will Turn Me	Buxtehude
Suite Gothique	Boellmann
Sarabande	Bach-Phillips
Rhosymedre ("Lovely")	Williams
O Perfect Love	Barnby

THE PROCESSIONAL HYMN "Love Divine, All Love Excelling" (*the* CONGREGATION *standing and singing*)

Sentences of Worship

MINISTER "It is not good that the man should be alone" (Genesis 2:18).

"Therefore a man leaves his father and his mother, and cleaves to his wife; and they become one flesh" (Genesis: 2:24).

The quality of love for all of life's relationships has been described by the Apostle Paul in his unforgettable words from his first letter to the Corinthians, Chapter 13: I may speak in tongues of men or of angels, but if I am without love, I am a sounding gong or a clanging cymbal. I may have the gift of prophecy, and know every hidden truth; I may have faith strong enough to move mountains; but if I have no love, I am nothing. I may dole out all I possess, or even give my body to be burnt, but if I have no love, I am none the better.

Love is patient; love is kind and envies no one. Love is never boastful, nor conceited, nor rude; never selfish, not quick to take offence. Love keeps no score of wrongs; does not gloat over other men's sins, but delights in the truth. There is nothing love cannot face; there is no limit to its faith, its hope, and its endurance.

Love will never come to an end. Are there prophets? their work will be over. Are there tongues of ecstacy? they will cease. Is there knowledge? it will vanish away; for our knowledge and our prophecy alike are partial, and the partial vanishes when wholeness comes. When I was a child, my speech, my outlook, and my thoughts were all childish. When I grew up, I had finished with childish things. Now we see only puzzling reflections in a mirror, but then we shall see face to face. My knowledge now is partial; then it will be whole, like God's knowledge of me. In a word, there are three things that last forever: faith, hope, and love; but the greatest of them all is love (NEB).

The Charge to the Congregation and the Couple

MINISTER   On this occasion _____ and _____ come before family, friends, and church to affirm the choice that they have made of each other as life mates. They declared their intention to establish a home for the raising of a family and the fulfillment of life together. How like the church in its relationship to its Lord is the wedding of two people. May you see in this relationship of Christ and His Church the pattern of love and devotion for husband and wife.

The Service of the Engagement Vows

MINISTER   In olden days the engagement service was performed on the church steps at the time of the announcement of the engagement of the couple. Later it was incorporated into the actual wedding service. In order to allow the bride and groom to go together to the altar, this portion of the service will be performed at the end of the main aisle opposite the altar.

(MINISTER *moves to the end of aisle and is met there by the* BRIDE *and* GROOM *with* PARENTS *and* WEDDING PARTY.)

MINISTER _____ (GROOM), will you take this woman as your wife, will you be faithful to her in tender love and honor, offering her encouragement and companionship; and will you live with her, and cherish her, as love and respect would lead you, in the bond of marriage?

GROOM   I will.

MINISTER _____ (BRIDE), will you take this man as your husband; and will you honor and respect him, will you give him strength and encouragement, will you love him and live with him as a mate, a companion, and a lover, and will you faithfully cherish him in the bonds of marriage?

BRIDE   I will.

MINISTER   Who gives this woman to marry this man?

FATHER OF BRIDE   Her mother and father do.

(*Having publicly declared their intention of marriage,* THE COUPLE *and the* WEDDING PARTY *will now proceed up the main aisle to the altar.*)

Meditation

MINISTER _____ and _____ as you contemplate the making of your vows to each other, realize that henceforth your destinies shall be woven of one design and your perils and your joys shall not be known apart. Today you are making public, for all to know, that the words, "I love you," are a full commitment of yourselves to each other, to the forsaking of all other lovers, and to the assuming of adult responsibility in society. Marriage has possibilities of failure and success as well as pain and joy, sorrow and happiness. The possibilities are greater in married life than in single life. You have declared your intention to make this venture of faith and love.

The Exchange of Wedding Vows

GROOM   I, _____, having full confidence that our abiding faith in each other as human beings will last our lifetime, take you, _____, to be my wedded wife; I promise to be your loving and faithful husband; in prosperity and in need, in joy and in sorrow, in sickness and in health, and to respect your privileges as an individual as long as we both shall live.

BRIDE   I, _____, having full confidence that our abiding faith in each other as human beings will last our lifetime, take you, _____, to be my wedded husband; I promise to be your loving and faithful wife; in prosperity and need, in joy and in sorrow, in sickness and in health, and wherever you go I will follow, and where you live, I will live, your people shall be my people and your God, my God for as long as we both shall live.

The Service of the Rings (*spoken by both in double ring ceremony*)   As this ring has no end, neither shall my love for you.

THE WEDDING PRAYER (MINISTER)   Eternal God, the spring of life and giver of spiritual grace; bless these our friends, that living together, they may fulfill the vows and covenant made between them. May they ever remain in perfect love and peace together according to Your Spirit in Jesus Christ, our Lord. Amen.

THE LORD'S PRAYER (*in unison*)   Our Father, who art in heaven, hallowed be Thy name. Thy kingdom come, Thy will be done, on earth as it is in heaven. Give us this day our daily bread. And forgive us our debts, as we forgive our debtors. And lead us not into temptation, but deliver us from evil. For Thine is the kingdom and the power and the glory, for ever. Amen.

The Declaration of Marriage

MINISTER   Since you have promised your love to each other, and before God and these witnesses have exchanged these solemn vows, as a minister of Jesus, I declare you to be husband and wife. What God has joined, let no one separate.

The Benediction

MINISTER   May the joy and peace which only God can give, and which cannot be taken away by anything in this world, be yours today and in all of life's tomorrows. Amen.

THE RECESSIONAL HYMN   "Now Thank We All Our God" (*the*
  CONGREGATION *standing and singing*)

THE POSTLUDE
  Hymn to Joy   Beethoven

OUTDOOR WEDDING SERVICE

*The setting for this service is a backyard or park, filled with
trees and flowers. The altar is a prie-dieu placed with the most
beautiful background. If held in the evening, torches or patio
lights are placed around the yard. Chairs may be formed around
the altar, or persons may stand throughout. The aisle to the altar
may be roped off by ribbon or be a carpet runner. Music for
the processional and wedding ceremony may be composed of
flute, violin, or guitars. As guests arrive they are each given a
flower; then, during the recessional, the flower petals are thrown
upon the* BRIDE *and* GROOM *as a "shower of blessings." The
reception takes place outdoors also, with tables set up opposite
the altar. During the reception a festive, celebrative, joyful mood
should prevail with swinging music, including drums, trumpet,
saxophone and strings. A balloon is given to each person as he
comes to the reception table.*

MINISTER   Friends, we are meeting here amid the beauty of
  nature and in the presence of God to unite this man _____
  and this woman _____, in marriage.

  Let us pray: Maker of all beauty, who makes the sun to
  rise in splendor, and to march in quiet radiance across the
  sky; who has filled the face of the earth with trees and flowers,
  birds and bees, who has given perfume to flowers, harmony
  to thought, holiness to character, we rejoice in Your perfection,

and in the marvelous design that unites us as families. You are all holy and beautiful. Teach us all to live in the beauty of Your holiness as known in Jesus, the Lord. Amen.

The occasion that declares publicly the intention of a man and a woman to enter into the relationship of love has become known in our society as a wedding. For the Christian, this occasion is not spectacle, but worship; it is not a mere formal observance, but a participation in the will of God for life. A wedding is the celebration of the highest we know in love, the pledging of the deepest fidelity, the expression of the highest aspiration. A relationship so sacred must not be entered into casually but thoughtfully and deliberately.

On this occasion _____ and _____ come before family and friends to affirm the choice that they have made of each other as a life's mate and their intention to establish a home for the raising of a family and the fulfillment of life together.

Let us pray: Out of this tangled world, O God, You have drawn together these two persons and are binding them firmly by the sure insights of love. We thank You for the homes in which _____ and _____ have been nurtured in the formative years of their lives; for parents who have sacrificed in their behalf and made possible opportunities of education; for the church which has awakened them to the meaning of eternal life. Look with favor upon their union and nurture its love with the Spirit of Jesus Christ. Amen.

Are you, _____ (GROOM) ready to enter this holy relationship, to accept the responsibilities of a husband; to be _____'s (BRIDE) loving, faithful, and helpful husband whether in days of success or adversity? (GROOM *answers:* "I am.")

Are you, _____ (BRIDE) ready to enter this holy relationship, to accept the responsibilities of a wife; to be _____'s (GROOM) loving, faithful and helpful wife whether in days of success or adversity? (BRIDE *answers:* "I am.")

By these answers, which you have given after due consideration and serious thought, your purpose and willingness to take one another for better or for worse from this day forward, is affirmed.

And now, who gives _____ (BRIDE) to be married to _____ (GROOM)? (*Both* PARENTS *answer:* "We, her mother and father do.")

And now, who gives _____ (GROOM) to be married to _____ (BRIDE)? (*Both* PARENTS *answer:* "We, his mother and father do.")

Now, if you know of nothing, legal or moral, to forbid your union and wish now to take its vows, indicate that by joining your right hands.

"And now I will show you the best way of all," admonished the Apostle Paul. "I may speak in tongues of men or of angels, but if I am without love, I am a sounding gong or a clanging cymbal. I may have the gift of prophecy, and know every hidden truth; I may have faith strong enough to move mountains; but if I have no love, I am nothing. I may dole out all I possess, or even give my body to be burnt, but if I have no love, I am none the better.

"Love is patient; love is kind and envies no one. Love is never boastful, nor conceited, nor rude; never selfish, not quick to take offence. Love keeps no score of wrongs; does not gloat over other men's sins, but delights in the truth. There is nothing love cannot face; there is no limit to its faith, its hope, and its endurance.

"Love will never come to an end. Are there prophets? their work will be over. Are there tongues of ecstasy? they will cease. Is there knowledge? it will vanish away; for our knowledge and our prophecy alike are partial, and the partial vanishes when wholeness comes. When I was a child, my speech, my outlook, and my thoughts were all childish. When I grew up, I had finished with childish things. Now we see only puzzling reflections in a mirror, but then we shall see face to face. My knowledge now is partial; then it will be whole, like God's knowledge of me. In a word, there are three things that last forever; faith, hope, and love, but the greatest of them all is love" (1 Corinthians 13 NEB).

You each have prepared your own covenant of love. Will you publicly vocalize that covenant to the other now?

GROOM *to* BRIDE   Learning from my parents' example, _____, I carry with me very special expectations of a kind of love that should be shared between two people. I believe I have found that kind of love in our relationship. Through you I have learned the joys derived from actively demonstrating my love for you through my life-style, rather than making empty verbal commitments. I have further been shown the powers of personal communication through which I have gained knowledge of myself, you, _____, and us. This ever-growing knowledge, which we must nurture throughout our lives will also lead to a more complete understanding of our families, friends, and neighbors. You, _____, by teaching me how to love, have also given me a sensitivity for life. Above all else we must preserve and strengthen our love for each other, for it is our love which is the key to any success we may hope for.

BRIDE *to* GROOM   _____, as we become united in marriage, I am thankful that I have come from a home in which love has had such a profound influence. Because of my family, I feel I am able to stand here today with a vision of what I hope for our future together. The most wonderful part of loving you, _____, has been discovering how beautiful the pronoun *we* can be. I hope that we will continue to grow together and yet at the same time encourage each other in our personal endeavors. From you I have begun to learn the real meaning of such qualities as patience, kindness, and serenity. Because of you I want to continue to learn more. My hand in yours is a symbol to me of my vision of our future, two individuals united by a strong bond of love, walking together, always in the same direction. I hope I can make for you a little corner, no matter where in the world it is, where we may live, love, and be kind.

MINISTER From the earliest time, the golden circle has been a symbol of wedded love. (MINISTER *receives rings from* BEST MAN *and* MAID-OF-HONOR.) It is made of pure gold to symbolize pure love. Being one unbroken circle, it symbolizes unending love. As often as either of you see these golden circles, you will be reminded of this high moment and the unending love you promise.

To GROOM Take this ring which you have selected, place it upon the finger of your bride and say to her these words: "With this ring I thee wed, in the name of the Father, and of the Son, and of the Holy Spirit."

To BRIDE Take this ring which you have selected, place it upon the finger of your groom and say to him these words: "This ring I give thee, in token and pledge of our constant faith and abiding love."

Since you have promised your love to each other, and before God and these witnesses have exchanged these solemn vows, and these symbols of genuine and undying love, as a minister of the Gospel of Jesus Christ, I recognize you as husband and wife. "What therefore God has joined together, let no man put asunder" (Matthew 19:6).

Let us kneel in prayer: Our Spiritual Father, grant to this couple true love to unite them spiritually, patience to assimilate their differences, forgiveness to cover their failures, guidance to lead them in the proper ways, courage to face perplexity, and inner peace to comfort and uphold them even in disillusionment and distress throughout their lives. In Jesus' Name. Amen.

May I present to you Mr. and Mrs. _____. Congratulations may be given at the reception.

CONGREGATION Peace be with you. (*As* COUPLE *leaves, flowers are thrown as the* CONGREGATION *speaks the blessing.*)

HOME WEDDING

Gathering music may be a medley of contemporary love songs played by guitars or, if necessary, recordings. An altar area with prie-dieu, flowers, and candelabra is arranged in the largest room. Flute music is light and joyful for the processional.

MINISTER   Married love has been, from the beginning of time, enshrined in dignity and honor. It is the bond wherein is realized the divine in human life.

It is not to be entered into flippantly nor temporarily, but only with integrity, personal commitment, and in Godly reverence and love.

Into this holy relationship, these two persons come now to be joined.

Let us pray: Eternal Father, whose very nature is love, look with favor upon these people who desire to make their vows of commitment, and who seek Your blessings and those of their families and friends, in the love of Jesus Christ our Lord. Amen.

We were made to love and to be loved. We walk this earth as unfinished creations until we find fulfillment in the love of others. Those of us who were fortunate found the greatest significance in our childhood lives when we were able to share our joys and fears, our triumphs and sorrows, in the love of parents and brothers and sisters. As our growing lives extended beyond the home, we found meaning and enrichment in the love of a few sincere friends. Emerging into maturity, the hunger of the lonely soul brings us to the greatest thing in human life, the love between man and woman. Here, we have the fusion of two personalities—a new creation—and human incompleteness has found divine fulfillment. As each of you sacrifices some freedom to the covenant between you, you will find greater freedom from loneliness and self-concern. As each of you pledges exclusive devotion to the other, you will find a flood of tenderness welling up within you which can become a passion for the welfare of all mankind. As each of you shares the innermost experiences with the other, you will find that God is dwelling in your midst. I am very happy for you, _____ and _____, for you have found the key that can unlock the universe to the hearts of men.

MINISTER (*to* GROOM) _____, will you have _____ to be your wedded wife, to live together after God's ordinance in the holy estate of matrimony?

GROOM   I will.

MINISTER (*to* BRIDE) _____, will you have _____ to be your wedded husband, to live together after God's ordinance in the holy estate of matrimony?

BRIDE   I will.

MINISTER   Who presents this bride in marriage?

FATHER OF BRIDE   Her mother and I do.

1 Corinthians, 13:4–7 (TEV)   Love is patient and kind; love is not jealous, or conceited, or proud; love is not ill-mannered, or selfish, or irritable; love does not keep a record of wrongs; love is not happy with evil, but is happy with the truth. Love never gives up; its faith, hope, and patience never fail.

GROOM   I, _____, accept you, _____, as my wedded wife to share in the fulness of Christian living as long as we both shall live.

BRIDE   I, _____, accept you, _____, as my wedded husband to share in the fulness of Christian living as long as we both shall live.

MINISTER   What symbol do you now exchange as an outward sign of your love?

Let us pray: O God, may these rings ever signify the love of these two. As these circles are fashioned without an ending, they speak of eternity. May the incorruptible substance of these rings represent a love glowing with increasing luster through the years. Amen.

GROOM With this wedding ring, I pledge my love and loyalty forever.

BRIDE With this wedding ring, I pledge my love and loyalty forever. Wherever you go, I will go, and wherever you dwell, I will dwell. (*optional*)

GROOM Your people shall be my people, and your God my God. (*optional*)

MINISTER Let us pray: O God, as You love these two, so may they love each other. In their new responsibilities, grant them the gift of warmth in all their relationships, the gift of common sense in meeting their problems, and the gift of communication in deepening their union, through the spirit of Jesus Christ. Amen.

Since _____ and _____ have exchanged their vows according to the laws of _____ and in the presence of this company, but more importantly in the Presence of God, I, with the authority invested in me as a minister of the Gospel of Jesus Christ, announce you to be husband and wife.

Will you kneel for the benediction?

Benediction

MINISTER May the Lord fill you with all spiritual benediction and grace that you may live together in the fulness of life.

May you have peace—
    Not of the stagnant pool, but of deep waters, flowing.
May you have poise—
    Not of the sheltered tree, but of the oak, deep rooted, storm strengthened, and free.
May you have power—
    Not of fisted might, but of the quickened seed stretching toward infinite light. Amen.

SOLO "One Hand—One Heart"

Symbolic Candle Lighting   (BRIDE *and* GROOM *rise, take the outside lighted candles of a three-pronged candelabrum, and together light the center candle, then extinguish the two outside candles.*)
MINISTER   ". . . It is not good that man should be alone . . . Therefore a man leaves his father and his mother, and cleaves to his wife, and they become one flesh" (Genesis 2:18, 24). As two lights are now blended into one, so two lives are blended into one.

May you be one in name, one in aim, and one in happy destiny together.

(GROOM *kisses the* BRIDE. *As couple turns, facing the congregation,* MINISTER *says:*)

I present Mr. and Mrs. _____. Congratulations are now in order.

The Kiss of Peace   (*Each person kisses the* BRIDE *and* GROOM *on the cheek and gives a personal blessing.*)

MARRIAGE AS A PART OF FORMAL WORSHIP [3]

A Prelude of Organ Music

Litanies	Alain
My Heart Is Ever Yearning	Brahms
Thou Art the Rock	Mulet
Sheep May Safely Graze	Bach
Adagio (Symphony VI)	Widor

The Greeting
MINISTER   When Jesus was invited with His disciples to the marriage in Cana, He gladly accepted the invitation, and there began His ministry of joy and His acts of power. So we

are assembled to share prayers and greetings with _____ and
_____ who come to make their vows in the midst of worship.

THE HYMN OF JOY   "All Creatures of Our God and King" (CON-
GREGATION *standing and singing*)

The Invocation (CONGREGATION *standing*)

MINISTER   May God be gracious to us and bless us in Jesus Christ
our Lord. Amen.

The Remembrance of The Mighty Acts of God   The Gospel
according to John, chapter 1:1–18.

A Confession of Who We Are

MINISTER   We have heard of the action of God in the past. Now
we know that we who live today are as fallible as those who
lived in the past. We fall short of the goal of full humanity as
we see it in Jesus the Christ. We stand in need of God's love,
thus we confess our state of being and call for forgiveness.

PEOPLE   Our Father, we confess our bondage to the present age.
We live as if no one had ever lived—had ever loved, had wept,
had thrilled to the touch of a friend, had grieved for a broken
relationship, had agonized over decisions, had given in to the
clutch of passion, had felt remorse or regret—before we came
into the world. Therefore, we have cut ourselves off from the
world and the wisdom that has been wrought out of the agony
and joy of past generations. Enable us to enter into a living
fellowship with the great souls of the past that they might give
us power for the present and the shaping of the future, especially the One whom we call the Christ. Amen.

An Affirmation of the Faith of the Church

MINISTER   Since the beginning, the Christian community has
found it important to declare the essentials of its faith in worship. It has done so in order that persons might constantly ex-
amine their own faith in light of that which is the community's.
Therefore, let us as the congregation of the People of God join
in such a statement.

PEOPLE   May we have the same attitude that Christ Jesus had.

Though He possessed the nature of God, He did not grasp at equality with God, but laid it aside to take on the nature of a slave and become like other men. When He had assumed human form, He still further humbled Himself and carried His obedience so far as to die, and to die upon the cross. That is why God has so greatly exalted Him, and given Him the name above all others, so that at the Name of Jesus everyone should kneel, and everyone should confess and acknowledge Jesus Christ as Lord, and thus glorify God the Father. Amen.

CHORAL RESPONSE   "Send Out Thy Light and Thy Truth"

THE CELEBRATION OF MARRIAGE

HYMN   "Be Thou My Vision, O Lord of My Heart" (CONGREGA-TION *standing and singing as wedding party proceeds to the front*)

MINISTER   As we gather here to witness and celebrate the marriage between _____ and _____ let us rejoice! (*to the* PARENTS) Believing that it is only out of families that new families emerge; and by your presence here affirming this fact: Do you _____ and _____ (BRIDE'S PARENTS' *names*) agree that your daughter, _____ should now be united in marriage with _____?

PARENTS   We do.

MINISTER   Do you _____ and _____ (GROOM'S PARENTS' *names*) agree that your son, _____ should now be united in marriage with _____?

PARENTS   We do.

MINISTER (*to the* BRIDE *and* GROOM) In light of these words signifying the blessing of your respective families, I ask you, _____ and _____, to come and participate in the Celebration of Marriage by the exchanging of vows and the giving of rings.

MINISTER   1 Corinthians 13. (*after the reading, to the* GROOM) Will you repeat after me: I, _____, accept you, _____, as my wife. I receive you into the responsibility of living a life in constant covenant relation to each other. I commit my life to you in the full realization of all the joys and triumphs, perils and sorrows that will come to us as we live together as husband and wife from this time forth. (*to the* BRIDE) Will you repeat after me: I, _____, accept you, _____, as my husband. I receive you into the responsibility of living a life in constant covenant relation to each other. I commit my life to you in the full realization of all of the joys and triumphs, perils and sorrows that will come to us as we live together as husband and wife from this time forth.

The Giving and Receiving of Rings (*As ring is placed on the* BRIDE's *finger, the* GROOM *will say,* "Wear this ring as a symbol of my covenant of love.")

(*As the ring is placed on the* GROOM's *finger, the* BRIDE *will say,* "Wear this ring as a symbol of my covenant of love.")

The Blessing Prayer
MINISTER   Bless, O Lord, these who wear these rings, that they may fulfill the sacred covenant between them made, in Christ's name. Amen.

MINISTER   On behalf of the Christian community, since _____ and _____ have in the presence of God and in the presence of you, their families and friends, covenanted themselves in marriage, I declare that they are husband and wife. Friends of the Community of Christ, may I present Mr. and Mrs. _____.

The Great Thanksgiving of the People of God
THE HYMN OF THANKSGIVING   "Now Thank We All Our God" (CONGREGATION *stands to sing the hymn while the* WEDDING PARTY *moves to seats. The* CONGREGATION *remains standing for the prayer.*)

MINISTER   Lift up your hearts.

PEOPLE   We lift them to the Lord.

MINISTER   Let us give thanks for God's glory.

PEOPLE   We give thanks, we rejoice in the glory of all creation.

MINISTER   All glory be to God, who sent His only Son into the world to be a man, born of a woman's womb, to die for us on a cross we made.

PEOPLE   He came for us. Help us to accept His coming.

MINISTER   He stood among us, a man, in our world, the place of conflict, and commanded us to remember His death, His life-giving death, until He comes in glory.

PEOPLE   We remember His death; we wait for His coming.

MINISTER   The night He was arrested, the Lord Jesus took bread, He gave thanks; He broke it, and gave it to His disciples saying, "Take, eat; this is my body. Do this in remembrance of me."

He also took the cup; He gave thanks; and gave it to them saying, "Drink of it, all of you; this is my blood of the covenant, which is poured out for many for the forgiveness of sins."

PEOPLE   Come, Lord Jesus, come.

MINISTER   Therefore, remembering His death, believing in His rising from the grave, yearning to recognize His presence; in this place, now, we obey His command; we offer bread and wine; we offer ourselves, to be used.

PEOPLE   Everything is Yours, O Lord; we return the gift You first gave us.

MINISTER   Accept our offering, O God. Send the spirit of life and power, glory and love, upon these people, this bread, this wine, that it may be to us His body and His blood now and always.

PEOPLE   Risen Lord, live in us that we may live in You.

MINISTER   Now with all men who ever were, who are, or ever shall be, with all creation in all time, we with joy sing:

ALL:

> Holy, Holy, Holy, Lord God Almighty
> All Thy works shall praise Thy name,
> In earth and sky and sea.
> Holy, Holy, Holy, Merciful and Mighty!
> God over all and blest eternally. Amen.

MINISTER   And now in His words, we say boldly: The Lord's Prayer. (*all*)

MINISTER   The things of God for the People of God.

PEOPLE   Amen.

The Communion of the People (*Emblems are distributed to worshipers who hold them until* MINISTER *leads in simultaneous participation.*)

MINISTER In the ancient Oriental world—within the home—a covenant rite, a personal pledge of loyalty was practiced by simply partaking of bread and drink. In that time, to break faith with one with whom one had broken bread was a most heinous sin. When loved ones were to be separated, they broke bread together as a pledge of love and loyalty, even at the sacrifice of body and blood.

Now as they were eating, Jesus took bread and blessed and broke it and gave it to the disciples and said, "Take; [eat,] this is my body . . . and he took a cup, and when he had given thanks he gave it to them . . . and said to them, "This is my blood of the covenant [of love] which is poured out for many [for the forgiveness of sins]."

The Benediction

MINISTER So this is love, Lord; not possession, but surrender; not indulgence, but sacrifice; not novelty, but constancy. Help this couple, O Lord, and all of us, with Your support, so that we may love throughout our lives, in Christ's Spirit. Amen.

HYMN "Rejoice Ye Pure in Heart" (*Verses 1 and 4 are sung by the standing* CONGREGATION *as the* WEDDING PARTY *departs.*)

THE POSTLUDE (*organ*) "Psalm 19"—Marcello

ROMAN CATHOLIC AND PROTESTANT SERVICE OF HOLY MATRIMONY [4]

The service may be used where one is a Roman Catholic and one a Protestant, with a clergyman from each participating in the service.

The Introductory Greeting   Dear friends, _____ and _____, you have come together in this church so that the Lord may seal and strengthen your love in the presence of the church's ministers and this community.

Opening Prayer   Father, we offer our prayers for _____ and _____, who have come here to be united in marriage before Your altar. Grant them Your blessing, and strengthen their love for each other, we ask in Jesus' name, Amen.

The Liturgy of the Word (*Choose three readings. All are from the Jerusalem Bible.*)   In the celebration of marriage, it is especially helpful to hear of the importance of marriage as recorded in the history of the Christian community.

In the Old Testament we read:

(1) God said, 'Let us make man in our own image, in the likeness of ourselves, and let them be masters of . . . the earth.'

> God created man in the image of himself,
> in the image of God he created him,
> male and female he created them.

. . . God saw all he had made, and indeed it was very good.

Genesis 1:26–28, 31

(2) [The Lord] God said, 'It is not good that the man should be alone. I will make him a helpmate.' . . . So the Lord God made the man fall into a deep sleep. And while he slept, he took one of his ribs and enclosed it in flesh. [Then the Lord] built the rib he had taken from the man into a woman, and brought her to the man. The man exclaimed:

> 'This at last is bone from my bones,
> and flesh from my flesh!
> This is to be called woman,
> for this was taken from man.'

This is why a man leaves his father and mother and joins himself to his wife, and they become one body.

Genesis 2:18–24

(3) Happy the husband of a really good wife;
    the number of his days will be doubled.
A perfect wife is the joy of her husband,
    he will live out the years of his life in peace.
A good wife is the best of portions,
    reserved for those who fear the Lord;
Rich or poor, they will be glad of heart,
    cheerful of face, whatever the season.
The grace of a wife will charm her husband,
    her accomplishments will make him the stronger.
A silent wife is a gift from the Lord,
    no price can be put on a well-trained character.
A modest wife is a boon twice over,
    a chaste character cannot be weighed on scales.
Like the sun rising over the mountains of the Lord
    is the beauty of a good wife in a well-kept house.
Like the lamp shining on the sacred lamp-stand
    is a beautiful face on a well-proportioned body.
Like golden pillars on a silver base
    are shapely legs on firm-set heels.

                        Ecclesiasticus 26:1–4, 16–21

In the New Testament record we read:

(1) Be ambitious for higher gifts. And I am going to show you
a way that is better than any of them.

    If I have all the eloquence of men or of angels, but speak
without love, I am simply a gong booming or a cymbal
clashing. If I have the gift of prophecy, understanding all
the mysteries there are, and knowing everything, and if I
have faith in all its fulness to move mountains, but without
love, then I am nothing at all. If I give away all that I
possess, piece by piece, and if I even let them take my
body to burn it, but am without love, it will do me no good
whatever.

    Love is always patient and kind; it is never jealous; love is
never boastful or conceited; it is never rude or selfish; it does
not take offence, and is not resentful. Love takes no pleasure
in other people's sins but delights in the truth; it is always

ready to excuse, to trust, to hope, and to endure whatever
comes.

Love does not come to an end. . . .

1 Corinthians 12:31–13:8

(2) My children,
our love is not to be just words or mere talk,
but something real and active;
only by this can we be certain
that we are children of the truth
and be able to quieten our conscience in his presence,
whatever accusations it may raise against us,
because God is greater than our conscience and he knows
everything.

1 John 3:18–20

(3) But from the beginning of creation God made them male
and female. This is why a man must leave father and
mother, and the two become one body. They are no longer
two, therefore, but one body. So then, what God has united,
man must not divide!

Mark 10:6–9

(4) [Jesus said to His disciples:]
This is my commandment:
love one another,
as I have loved you.
A man can have no greater love
than to lay down his life for his friends.
You are my friends,
if you do what I command you.

John 15:12–16

The Homily You are now standing before relatives, friends,
and clergy to promise to share your lives together, "until death
do you part." This is a permanent commitment to love and honor
one another in good times and in bad, in poverty and in plenty,
in sickness and in health, for better or for worse. These are
serious words and solemn vows—too serious for some who merely
live together without commitment, with relationships no more
binding than their own flippancy or selfish motivation. The

rising divorce rate indicates the unwillingness to persevere when difficulties arise.

The joy of marriage is the sense of security which goes with a feeling of being loved and wanted and needed, a realization that someone cares for us—on a permanent basis. One young lady remarked that her goal in life is to love and understand, to be loved and understood. She seeks it in that intimate relationship with the man who will be by her side until death.

A marriage that lasts for life demands love and loyalty, trust and unselfishness, God's grace and peace.

The Rite of Marriage

THE INTENTION Dear friends, as Christ blessed the marriage feast of Cana, so He will abundantly enrich and strengthen your love as you assume its duties in mutual and lasting fidelity. In the presence of God and the Church, I ask you to declare your intention:

_____ and _____, have you come here freely and without reservation to give yourselves to each other in marriage? (*Each answers:* "I have.")

Will you love and honor each other as husband and wife for the rest of your lives? (*Each answers:* "I will.")

Will you accept children lovingly from God, and bring them up according to the teaching of Christ and His Church? (*Each answers:* "I will."—*This question may be eliminated with those advanced in years.*)

THE CONSENT Who gives approval for this woman to enter this marriage relationship?

FATHER OF THE BRIDE Her mother and I do.

CLERGYMAN Since it is your intention to enter into marriage, join your right hands, and declare your consent before God and His Church. (*They move to prie-dieu. The* BRIDEGROOM *and* BRIDE *may memorize the vows or repeat phrases after* CLERGYMAN.)

GROOM I, _____, take you, _____, to be my wife. I promise to be true to you in good times and in bad, in sickness and in health. I will love you and honor you all the days of my life.

BRIDE   I, _____, take you, _____, to be my husband. I promise to be true to you in good times and in bad, in sickness and in health. I will love you and honor you all the days of my life.

(*Or, if deemed preferable, the consent may be obtained through questions: First to the* BRIDEGROOM) _____, do you take _____ to be your wife? Do you promise to be true to her in good times and in bad, in sickness and in health, to love her and honor her all the days of your life? (*The* BRIDE-GROOM *says:* I do.)

CLERGYMAN (*to the* BRIDE) _____, do you take _____ to be your husband? Do you promise to be true to him in good times and in bad, in sickness and in health, to love him and honor him all the days of your life? (*The* BRIDE *says:* I do.)

CLERGYMAN   You have declared your consent before the Church. May the Lord in His Goodness strengthen your consent and fill you both with His Spirit. What God has joined, men must not divide.

EXCHANGE OF RINGS   May the Lord bless these rings which you give to each other as the sign of your love and fidelity. May these rings always remind you of your love for and faith in each other.

The BRIDEGROOM *places his* BRIDE's *ring on her finger and says to her* _____, take this ring as a sign of my love and fidelity. In the name of the Father, and of the Son, and of the Holy Spirit.

The BRIDE *places her* BRIDEGROOM's *ring on his finger and says to him* _____, take this ring as a sign of my love and fidelity. In the name of the Father, and of the Son and of the Holy Spirit.

CLERGYMAN   My dear friends, let us turn to the Lord and pray that He will bless with His grace _____ and _____, who are now married, in the name of Christ.

THE BLESSING   Let us pray together: The Lord's Prayer (*in unison*).

May the Lord bless you with many happy years together, so that you may enjoy the rewards of a good life. And after you have served Him loyally in His kingdom on earth, may He welcome you to His eternal kingdom in heaven. Amen.

AN INTERFAITH CEREMONY

This service is designed for young people of different religious traditions such as Protestant and Roman Catholic, Episcopal and Free Church, Christian and non-Christian. It presumes participation by two clergymen, with the bride's minister as host.

The service therefore is designed to include portions familiar to most every tradition, including Protestant, Roman Catholic, Orthodox, and Jewish. An attempt has been made to couch the service in a contemporary flavor. Also effort has been made to exclude what might be offensive to various traditions.

PROCESSIONAL   "Greensleeves"

Call to Worship

HOST MINISTER   Friends, we are gathered together in the sight of God, within the presence of this company to join together _____ and _____ in holy matrimony. It is an honorable estate, instituted of God, and symbolizing the concern of the community of mankind in the covenant which they are now about to make.

"In the beginning God created the heavens and the earth. . . . Then God said, 'Let us make man in our image. . . .' So God created man . . . in the image of God created he him; male and female he created them. . . . Then the Lord said, 'It is not good that man should be alone. . . .' Therefore a man leaves his father and his mother and cleaves to his wife, and they become one flesh" (Genesis 1:1; 26; 27; 2:18; 24).

From the beginning, He blessed their union and asked by their love, they bring new life to the earth, and thereby share in His creation.

CONGREGATION   Amen.

The Invocation

HOST MINISTER   "O Lord, our Lord—

CONGREGATION   How excellent is Your name in all the earth. . . ."

HOST MINISTER   O Lord, hear my prayer,

CONGREGATION   And let my cry come to You.

HOST MINISTER   The Lord be with you—

CONGREGATION   And with your spirit.

HOST MINISTER   Let us pray: Direct, O Lord, we ask You, all our actions by Your inspiration. And carry them on by Your assistance, that every prayer and work of ours may always begin from You and through You be brought to completion, in Your holy Name.

CONGREGATION   Amen.

HYMN (optional)   "Praise to the Lord" (two verses)

The Declaration of Intention

OTHER CLERGYMAN (or other religious leader)   From the dawn of human history, it has been customary for the group to put the seal of public approval upon the union of man and woman. By the loving devotion and sacrifice of innumerable men and women through the long ages, this relationship has been purified and ennobled, until married love has become a center of clearest realization of the divine in human life.

It is therefore not to be entered into unadvisedly or lightly, but discreetly and in the love of God.

In this holy estate, these two persons come now to be joined.

OTHER CLERGYMAN   Who presents this bride in marriage?

FATHER OF BRIDE   Her mother and I do.

OTHER CLERGYMAN   This union in which you are about to enter will influence your whole future. That future, with its joys and disappointments, successes and failures, pleasures and pains, is hidden from your eyes. Not knowing what is before you, you come now to take each other for better or for worse, for richer or for poorer, in sickness and in health, until death parts you.

OTHER CLERGYMAN (*to* GROOM) _____ will you have _____ to be your wedded wife, to live together after God's ordinance in the holy estate of matrimony, according to the holy rite of the Church of God?

GROOM I will.

OTHER CLERGYMAN (*to* BRIDE) _____ will you have _____ to be your wedded husband, to live together after God's ordinance in the holy estate of matrimony, according to the holy rite of the Church of God?

BRIDE I will.

LORD'S PRAYER (*in unison*)

1 CORINTHIANS 13:4–7 (*paraphrased*) Love is patient and kind; love is not jealous, or conceited, or proud, love is not ill-mannered, or selfish, or irritable . . . love does not keep a record of wrongs; love is not happy with evil, but is happy with the truth. Love never gives up; its faith, hope, and patience never fail.

Sealing of the Marriage Bond

HOST MINISTER Now, join your right hands and speak your vows.

GROOM I, _____, accept you, _____, as my wedded wife to share in the fulness of living as long as we both shall live, because I love you very much.

BRIDE I, _____, accept you, _____, as my wedded husband to share in the fulness of living as long as we both shall live, because I love you very much.

Blessing the Wedding Rings

OTHER CLERGYMAN As a symbol of your constant and abiding love and of being joined together in holy marriage you will give and receive a ring. (*Rings given to the* CLERGYMAN.)

OTHER CLERGYMAN   The Lord be with you,

CONGREGATION   And with your spirit.

OTHER CLERGYMAN   Let us pray: Bless, O Lord, these rings so that those who wear them, keeping faith with each other in unbroken loyalty, may ever remain constant in mutual love and be at peace according to Your will and spirit.

CONGREGATION   Amen.

OTHER CLERGYMAN   Now that you have sealed your wedding covenant, give these wedding rings to each other.

GROOM   _____, take and wear this ring as a sign of our marriage vows.

BRIDE   _____, take and wear this ring as a sign of our marriage vows.

Confirmation of the Marriage Bonds

HOST MINISTER   By the authority of the church, I ratify and bless the bond of marriage you have contracted. In the name of the Father, and of the Son, and of the Holy Spirit.

CONGREGATION   Amen.

HOST MINISTER   I call upon all of you, here present, to be witnesses of this holy union which I have now blessed. "Man must not separate what God has joined together."

CONGREGATION   What, therefore, God has joined together, let no man put asunder.

HOST MINISTER   Let us kneel in prayer: Eternal God, whose grace promises all things, strengthen _____ and _____ with the gift of Your Holy Spirit, that they may fulfill the vows they have taken. Help them to keep faithful to each other and to You. Fill them with such love and joy so that when misunderstandings, irritations, and temptations occur, they may be quick to forgive, generous in patience, and dependably strong. Grant them fulness of years so that they may reap the harvest of the good life. Guide them by the counsel of Your Word. When their earthly life is complete, give to them Your eternal dominion in the unity of peace, forever and forever.

CONGREGATION   Amen.

UNISON PRAYER (*both* CLERGYMEN *and married* COUPLE)

> Lord, make us instruments of your peace;
> Where there is hatred, let us sow love;
> Where there is injury, pardon;
> Where there is doubt, faith;
> Where there is despair; hope;
> Where there is darkness, light;
> Where there is sadness, joy.
> O Divine Master, grant that we may not so much seek to
> be consoled, as to console; to be loved as to love; to
> be understood as to understand.
> For it is in giving that we receive; it is in pardoning
> that we are pardoned; and it is in dying that we are born
> to eternal life.

ST. FRANCIS OF ASSISI, *paraphrased*

Benediction

OTHER CLERGYMAN May the peace of God dwell in your hearts and in your home. May you have true friends to stand by you, both in joy and in sorrow. May you be strong in the grace and love, now and forever. Amen.

Symbolic Candle Lighting (BRIDE *and* GROOM *take the outside lighted candles of a three-pronged candelabrum, and together light the center candle, then extinguish the two outside candles.*)

HOST MINISTER "It is not good that the man should be alone. . . . Therefore a man leaves his father and his mother, and cleaves to his wife, and they become one flesh" (Genesis 2:18, 24). As two lights are now blended into one, so two lives are blended into one.

May you be one in name, one in aim, and one in happy destiny together.

(GROOM *kisses the* BRIDE. *As* COUPLE *turns, facing the congregation*)

HOST MINISTER I present Mr. and Mrs. _____

RECESSIONAL "Trumpet Voluntary in D"—Purcell

Section 5

SMALL GROUP
EXPERIMENTS

Section 5

SMALL GROUP
EXPERIMENTS

JOYFUL NOISE SERVICE

The theme stresses the presence of God in all life and the need to take all things God has created with thanksgiving. While gathering, electronic music is played.

Call to Worship

LEADER . . . Let us make a joyful noise to the rock of our salvation (Psalm 95:1).

WORSHIPERS Clap and shout, "Hallelujah! Praise be to God!"

LEADER Hear and see—and be thankful! (*Sounds taped from everyday life or from records or a cassette are played at random—beginning with a jet airplane taking off, a crowd at a football game, a rooster crowing, a baby crying, a Ping-Pong game, city traffic, an ambulance, a train passing, wind whistling, etc. The volume is reduced during the parts of service spoken by individuals.*

Simultaneous with the recording, slides are shown changing automatically every eight seconds. The slides might include people, civic buildings, a funeral, children playing, paintings, churches, landscapes, hospitals, Statue of Liberty, etc.)

CONGREGATION (*spontaneous comments or prayers of thanksgiving, confession, intercession as suggested by sounds and sights*)

The Lord's Supper (*When the tape recording begins playing, "Alleluia, Sing to Jesus," The* CONGREGATION *joins in singing. A slide of a contemporary painting of Jesus remains on the wall or screen during the Communion service.*)

The Word

LEADER "What God Has Done in Christ" (*reading from Acts 13:32, 33; John 1:1–4, 14. The* LEADER *emphasizes God's gift of Himself to us in Jesus, explicit in the Lord's Supper.*)

LEADER Be thankful for this gift as you come forward to partake of the emblems.

HYMN "This Is Me . . . for You"

NURSING HOME SERVICE

Give to each person coming to the worship service a button to wear with a SMILE—GOD LOVES YOU *slogan. Take a banner or two for the gathering area with slogans such as,* LOVE LIFE, CELEBRATE, CHOOSE LIFE, GOD IS LOVE, GOD LOVES YOU . . . SMILE.

A song service is conducted with guitars, using all kinds of gospel hymns, popular radio religious songs, with special-request time.

There should also be a time for Scripture recitation of favorite Biblical passages.

Prayers of Intercession for persons and concerns mentioned. (Procedures possible: Each person's name is put on a piece of paper, placed in a box. Then each person draws out a name for whom he or she prays; or, concerns may be called out orally and the LEADER *prays; or, sentence prayers may be given by those who wish from among the worshipers.)*

Meditation   *(brief, not more than six minutes)*

THE TOUCH OF LOVE

Do you believe God loves you? Do You? Do you feel God's love permeating your being?

The way to get past the far-away, stern, warlike God of the Old Testament is to begin with Christ. This button I am wearing says, SMILE—GOD LOVES YOU. Love Christ and enjoy God. It's as simple as that!

Christ came to show us a tender, loving, concerned, and forgiving God. Christ knew how to love people and this love is the essence of God.

Have you ever felt abused, neglected, unwanted, extra baggage? Have you been filled with resentment and bitterness? You need to love and to be loved in return.

When a child is ill, injured, or scared by a thunderstorm or a bad dream, he seeks a parent. He wants to be held, touched, or snuggled up. Human contact!

Jesus always touched the persons He healed. There is an outflowing from one person to another in the human touch. A woman, afflicted by bleeding, reached out just to touch the robe Jesus was wearing. In the contact, she was healed.

Try an experiment. Turn to the person nearest you. Put your hands together, as though for prayer. Let your neighbor put his or her hands over yours. Then let the person with hands on the outside say, "God bless you!"

Did you feel it? It's more powerful than words. It's the touch of love. Touch is important.

When God decided to give us Christmas, to commemorate His love for us, He did it with touch. He sent His Son, in human form, to touch us. That's why everything important in the church—baptism, receiving new members, ordination, healing, the touch is important. Love is communicated in touch!

An Alternate Meditation

"LENGTH OF DAYS" [1]

"Length of days" was thought to be a peculiar and cherished blessing promised to Abraham, David, Job and untold millions. Who among us does not agree? Why else do we strive to prolong life?

Long life multiplies the opportunities for service in glorifying God. When a person's life is prematurely cut short, what a shame! I am thinking of Raphael, the artist, who died in his thirties; of Jesus Christ, who was murdered at the age of thirty-three; of thousands of military boys, whose lives have been snuffed out in young adulthood; of children, whose potentials never had a chance to blossom. What tragedy! How unfortunate! What loss to the world! What a privilege to live to full age. Think of the mature judgment, usefulness, and labor of many years. Think of the accomplishments of those in sunset years.

Titian painted his masterpiece *The Battle of Lapanto* at the age of ninety-eight, Verdi wrote his great opera *Otello* at seventy-four, and *Falstaff* at eighty. Kant, at seventy-four, wrote his anthropology; Edison built chemical plants after he was sixty-seven; General MacArthur was Supreme Commander of the occupation in Japan in his seventies. Socrates learned to play a musical instrument in his old age; Canto, at eighty, studied Greek; Plutarch, almost as old, studied Latin. Dr. Samuel Johnson applied himself to the Dutch language only a few years before his death; yet one morning in later life, he amused himself by committing to memory eight hundred lines of *Virgil;* at the age of seventy-three, while suffering from an attack of paralysis so severe that it rendered him speechless, he composed a Latin prayer in order to test the condition of his mental facilities. Chaucer's *Canterbury Tales* were the composition of his later years. They were begun in his forty-seventh year and finished in his sixty-first. Franklin's *Philosophical Pursuits* began when he had nearly reached his fiftieth year. Sir Christopher Wren retired from public life at eighty-six; after that he spent five years in literary, astronomical, and religious pursuits. Necker offers a beautiful instance of the influence of late studies in life when he tells us, "The era of three scores and ten is an agreeable age for writing; your mind has not lost its vigor, and envy leaves you in peace."

(*Following the Meditation, have a moment when each person touches the other persons near him with the words,* "God loves you, and I love you.")

HOUSE PRAYER MEETING

Informally a group of four couples meets in someone's home. Presumably they know one another and meet frequently as a prayer group.

Bible Discussion *Bibles in different translations have been brought so each person has a Bible. A* LEADER, *chosen in advance, has made some preparation. Bible verses are read about a particular subject and facets of the subject. Each verse is read, in several translations if it seems desirable. Brief background comment is made by the one prepared. Others comment upon what relevance is implied today. All comments should be brief, with no one dominating the discussion, and no debating or arguing.*

Testimonies *When the Bible study is completed, each expresses, "This good thing happened to me this week. . . ."*

Conversational Prayer *Following the testimonies, concerns for prayer are mentioned to the group. After this two groups of four go to separate rooms for Conversational Prayer. Sitting in a circle close enough to hold hands, the persons pray spontane-*

ously for the particular concerns, and others that come to mind while in prayer. Prayers of thanksgiving conclude the prayer time.

Hymn Sing *Informal hymn singing may follow. The evening may be concluded with light refreshments, if desired.*

SENSITIVITY EXERCISE

Provide each one attending a pencil and list of the following incomplete sentences. Instruct the group to make a complete sentence of each, expressing their truest feelings. Allow approximately thirty minutes for this exercise.

1. I am happiest	11. Sports . . . .
2. Other people	12. Most women . . . .
3. My greatest fear is	13. I love . . . .
4. At night	14. I secretly . . . .
5. Men	15. Mother . . . .
6. Women	16. My greatest ambition . . . .
7. I hate	17. Church membership . . . .
8. I	18. My church . . . .
9. People	19. My minister . . . .
10. Dancing	20. Christ . . . .

Following the completion of these, each one shares (if he or she wishes) the answers to the first sentence. When each has done so, it may be analyzed and discussed. Then, the group does the same with the next—and so on, until the list is completed or time runs out.

The meeting may conclude with a devotion on "Christian Feelings," and sharing prayers about Christian Relationships.

Suggested Devotional on Christian Feelings Growing deeply inside all of us is the hunger for authentic life; and a distaste for sham and phoniness. There is a deep admiration for the person who is aware and sensitive to other's feelings which gives life a dimension of meaning.

The apprehension that life at its core does not make sense, does not add up, prevents us from fully functioning as human beings. Deeper than our anxiety over guilt or death is our anxiety over emptiness and meaninglessness.

Jesus is the personification of authentic life. In our Lord's Prayer, He gives us the feelings and attitudes we need to cultivate.

I cannot say . . . "Our"—if my religion has no room for other people and their needs.

I cannot say . . . "Father"—if I do not demonstrate this relationship in my daily life.

I cannot say . . . "Who art in Heaven"—if all my interests and pursuits are earthly things.

I cannot say . . . "Hallowed be Thy Name"—if I who am called by His name, am not holy.

I cannot say . . . "Thy kingdom come"—if I am unwilling to give up my sovereignty and accept the reign of God.

I cannot say . . . "Thy will be done"—if I am unwilling or resentful of having Him in my life.

I cannot say . . . "on earth as it is in Heaven"—unless I am truly ready to give myself to His service here and now.

I cannot say . . . "Give us this day our daily bread"— without expending honest effort for it or by ignoring the needs of my fellowmen.

I cannot say . . . "Forgive us our debts as we forgive our debtors"—if I continue to harbor a grudge against anyone.

I cannot say . . . "Lead us not into temptation"—if I deliberately choose to remain in a situation where I am likely to be tempted.

I cannot say . . . "Deliver us from evil"—if I am not prepared to fight in the spiritual realm with the weapon of prayer.

I cannot say . . . "Thine is the Kingdom, the Power, the Glory"—if I do not give disciplined obedience, if I fear what neighbors and friends may say or do, if I seek my own glory first.

I cannot say . . . "Amen"—unless I can honestly say also, cost what it may, this is my prayer! [2]

THANKSGIVING SERVICE FOR NEW BABY

This may be held in the hospital or at home. The MINISTER *makes an appointment to conduct the service when the entire family is present. Worship center: rosebud and vase are brought by the* MINISTER *and left with the family.*

Opening Words

MINISTER   The Psalmist expresses the feelings we harbor with the gift of this new life. "Lo, [children] are a heritage from the Lord. . . . Like arrows in the hand of a warrior are the sons of one's youth. Happy is the man who has his quiver full of them!" (Psalm 127:3, 4, 5).

What a joyful privilege is yours. God has said, "I'll lend you for a little while, a child of Mine, for you to love while he lives . . ." May your response be, "Dear Lord, for all the joy Your child shall bring, the risk of grief we'll run. We will shelter him with tenderness. We will love him while we may."

God has given you the privilege of parenthood. He has placed into your care and responsibility this helpless life. How mysterious is birth and life. What a blending and intertwining of life streams have occurred here. The directions this child shall take mentally, physically, socially, and spiritually will to a large measure be determined by you parents.

If your child could now take voice, (he or she) might say:
I have come into your world about which I know nothing.
Why I come I know not;
How I came I know not. . . .

You hold in your hand my destiny.
You determine, largely, whether I shall succeed or fail.
Give me, I pray you, those things that make for happiness.
Train me, I beg you, that I may be a blessing to the world.[3]

Let us pray to God.

Divine Source of life and spirit; we bow in thankfulness and awe before the mystery of this life. We bow in thankfulness for this new person, and for the privilege these two have of being its parents. Give to them maturity of judgment, self-control, and responsibility that they may please You. Grant the child a sound spirit that he may become Christlike and bring honor to our Lord and His Kingdom throughout his life. In Jesus' Name. Amen.

(*Picture taken of* FATHER, MOTHER *and* BABY; *placed in a beautiful folder from church, to be given to family, and an enrollment card for* BABY *in Nursery Department. Get information while there. Congratulations offered by* MINISTER, *then departure.*)

HOME SERVICE OF THANKSGIVING

This family service is especially appropriate on Thanksgiving Day. Table centerpiece is a cornucopia with all kinds of fruits, symbolizing the bountiful blessings received from God. Banners prepared in advance are placed on a mobile standard or tacked on the wall with such words as, THANK YOU GOD; WE CELEBRATE BEING ALIVE; JOY IS OURS; THANK GOD FOR TROUBLES TOO. *When dinner is ready, the family gathers around the table in room where food is served. Banners are brought in.*

HOST   How glad we are to be alive today. God has been good to all of us. Even in our troubles we have found meaning. We are so thankful—so let us celebrate:

BANNER HOLDER #1   We celebrate being alive. (*comments*)

BANNER HOLDER #2   We celebrate because joy is ours. (*comments*)

BANNER HOLDER #3   We thank God even for our troubles. (*comments*)

BANNER HOLDER #4   Thank You God! (*Thanksgiving Prayer*)

SONG (*played on recorder or sung by all*)   "Bless This House," or the "Doxology."

FAMILY HAPPY-TIME SERVICE

Before the evening meal (or before bedtime), the family meets together. Each family member tells, "What made me happy today . . . ."

Following the expressions, they all hold hands, forming a family circle. One person in the family (a different one each time) prays, "Thank You God for this good day." *During the meal, the experiences can be discussed further, or devotions, Bible study, or family discussion can follow.*

This simple procedure could become a weekly, or even daily routine.

DEDICATION OF A HOME

Start with an open-house social time. Then, with everyone congregating in the largest area, the service begins. The family's MINISTER *conducts the service with the family members participating. All the participants gather in front of the worship center. Here place a seven-branch candelabrum.*

Invitation

MOTHER or FATHER   Friends, we have invited you here to share with our family in the dedication of our home. We are glad you have come. We invite now your participation in this worship service. "Anyone can build an altar; it requires a God to provide the flame. Anybody can build a house; we need the Lord for the creation of a home." [4]

HYMN   "For the Beauty of the Earth" (*verses 1 and 4*).

PRAYER   God, our Heavenly Father, who has placed Your children in family units where love is to be nurtured and duty made sacred; we are thankful for this home of shelter and affection. Grant that this may be a school where each might become prepared for the high and holy tasks of life. Save it from the influences that destroy and degrade human personality. May this home be the antechamber to the larger household of God, and a foretaste of our true eternal home, now and evermore, in Jesus' Name. Amen.

SCRIPTURE READING   Matthew 7:24–27

Dedication of Family Room

MINISTER   What is a home? A roof to keep out the rain. Four walls to keep out the wind. Floors to keep out the cold. Yes, but home is more than that. It is the laugh of a baby, the song of a mother, the strength of a father. Warmth of loving hearts, light from happy eyes, kindness, loyalty, comradeship. Home is the first school and first church for young ones, where they learn what is right, what is good, and what is kind. Where they go for comfort when they are hurt or sick. Where joy is shared and sorrow eased. Where fathers and mothers are respected and loved. Where children are wanted.[5]

MEMBER OF FAMILY (*after lighting one candle*) We dedicate the family room to family relaxation, love, understanding, comfort, and activities.

Dedication of Living Room

MINISTER The beauty of a home is harmony, the security of a house is loyalty, the joy of a house is love, the rule of a house is service, the comfort of a house is in contented spirits. The real home is a place of real living.

MEMBER OF FAMILY (*after lighting another candle*) We dedicate the living room of this house as a place of joyful conversations, harmony, comfort, and love.

Dedication of Kitchen and Dining Room

MINISTER Thomas Wolfe said, "There is no spectacle on earth more appealing than that of a beautiful woman in the act of cooking dinner for someone she loves." Elton Trueblood writes, "The table is really the family altar. Here those of all ages come together and help to sustain both their physical and spiritual existence. It entwines the material and the spiritual in a re-markable way. The food, in and of itself, is purely physical, but it represents human service in its use. Here, at one common table, is the father who has earned, the mother who has pre-pared or planned, and the children who share, according to need. When we realize how deeply a meal together can be a spiritual and regenerating experience we can understand some-thing of why our Lord when He broke bread with His little company . . . told them, as often as they did it, to remember him. . . ."[6]

MEMBER OF FAMILY (*after lighting another candle*) We dedicate this kitchen and dining room to physical renewal, to family fellowship, and to spiritual memory and hope.

Dedication of Bedrooms

MINISTER Home is the one place in this world where hearts are
sure of each other. It is the place of confidence. It is the place
where we tear off that mask of guarded and suspicious coldness
which the world forces us to wear in self-defense, and where
we pour out the unreserved communications of full and con-
fiding hearts. It is the spot where expressions of tenderness
gush out without any sensation of awkwardness and without
any dread of ridicule.[7]

MEMBER OF FAMILY (*after lighting another candle*) We dedicate the bedrooms to rest, refreshment, and privacy.

Dedication of Library

MINISTER A person becomes what he reads! Henry Ward Beecher
said, "A little library growing larger each year is an honorable
part of a young man's history. It is man's duty to have books.
A library is not a luxury but one of the necessaries of life."
Mind is the master power that molds and makes. And man is
mind. Evermore he takes the tools of thought, and shaping
what he wills, brings forth a thousand joys or a thousand ills.

MEMBER OF FAMILY (*after lighting another candle*) We dedicate the library to the mental development of our entire family.

Dedication of Total Home

MINISTER Rufus Jones, the great Quaker, said, "I am most of all
thankful for my birthplace and early nurture in the warm
atmosphere of a spiritually-minded home, with a manifest touch
of saintliness in it; thankful, indeed, that from the cradle I was
saturated with the Bible and immersed in an environment of
religion, of experience, and reality. It was a peculiar grace that
I was born into that great inheritance of spiritual wisdom and
faith, accumulated through generations of devotion and sacri-
ficial love. I can never be grateful enough for what was done

for me by my progenitors before I came on the scene. They produced the spiritual atmosphere of my youth. I became heir of a vast invisible inheritance. There is nothing I would exchange for that." [8]

MEMBER OF FAMILY (*after lighting another candle*)   We dedicate our total home to the personal development of each member, and to the Christian responsibility of being a force for righteousness and love in the larger community.

Dedication of the Family Members

MINISTER   I charge each one of you as family members to put faith in the place of friction, to practice tolerance and understanding of others. Make this home worthy of the presence of Jesus the Unseen Guest. Let Him be your guide in speech and conduct. Dedicate each day's activities to the glory of God. Reinforce the work of the church. Be conscious of the wider brotherhood of man and the unity in God. Thus, you will find meaning in your home, strength to face the suffering, frustrations, and sorrows of life, and a foretaste of your eternal home.

FAMILY MEMBERS (*as one lights the final candle, in unison*)   We dedicate ourselves, in the Name of God the Father, God the Son, and God the Holy Spirit. Amen.

SOLO   "Bless This House"

Section 6

OUTDOOR WORSHIP OCCASIONS

Section 6

OUTDOOR WORSHIP OCCASIONS

DEAR EARTH—HANDLE WITH CARE [1]

This ecology service may be held indoors or outdoors.

Welcome

LEADER The earth is the Lord's and the fulness thereof—

PEOPLE The world and those who dwell therein.

LEADER Good morning!

PEOPLE Good morning!

LEADER Welcome to another week on the Planet Earth!

PEOPLE We've come to thank God for the privilege of being here.

LEADER Privilege? What's so great about living on this threatened globe?

PEOPLE We can recycle ourselves through Christ and then it will become a more liveable place.

LEADER I see, now I understand; that really is something to celebrate!

Greetings

LEADER Stand up and greet the people around you and anybody else you might like to greet this morning.

LET'S SING "This Is My Father's World"

174

LET'S PRAY   God of air, blow the smog of false desires out of our lungs, and replace it with the wind of Your Spirit. God of ocean and all waters, wash the synthetics out of our blood and replace them with our own true chemistry. God of the earth of decay and rebirth, break down the chlorinated hydrocarbons in our flesh, and let us live together with all other flesh. God of fire of the sun, blunt the needles of drugs and replace them with the desire of life.

Brothers and sisters, let us take up the loads of our common task. As we shake off from our feet the dust of the City of Destruction, let us turn our eyes to the New Jerusalem, and consecrate that Temple whose pillars have come alive as the forest cathedral. Let us be on our way, off the road, to the city whose street is a river of living waters, where the tree of life is blooming, and its leaves are for the healing of the nations. For God's sake and ours, Amen.

CHOIR—A SONG OF HOPE   "I'd Like To Teach the World To Sing"

PICTURE STORY

"Genesis—Last Chapter"

In the end, there was Earth, and it was with form and beauty. And man dwelt upon the lands of the earth, the meadows and trees, and he said, "Let us build our dwellings in this place of beauty." And he built cities and covered the Earth with concrete and steel. And the meadows were gone.

And man said, "It is good."

On the second day, man looked upon the waters of the Earth, and man said, "Let us put our wastes in the water that the dirt will be washed away," and man did. And the waters became polluted and foul in their smell.

And man said, "It is good."

On the third day, man looked upon the forests of the Earth and saw they were beautiful. And man said, "Let us cut the timber for our homes and grind the wood for our use." And man did. And the land became barren and the trees were gone.

And man said, "It is good."

On the fourth day, man saw that animals were in abundance and ran in the fields and played in the sun. And man said, "Let us cage these animals for our amusement and kill them for our sport." And man did. And there were no more animals on the face of the Earth.

And man said, "It is good."

On the fifth day man breathed the air of the Earth. And man said, "Let us dispose of our wastes into the air for the winds shall blow them away." And man did. And the air became filled with the smoke and the fumes could not be blown away. And the air became heavy with dust and choked and burned.

And man said, "It is good."

On the sixth day man saw himself; and seeing the many languages and tongues, he feared and hated. And man said, "Let us build great machines and destroy these lest they destroy us." And man built great machines and the Earth was fired with the rage of great wars.

And man said, "It is good."

On the seventh day man rested from his labors, and the Earth was still for man no longer dwelt upon the Earth.

And it was good.[2]

(*By photographing various aspects of the environment in their area—both the good and the bad—groups can assemble a slide series which can be most effective when accompanied by a narration of* "Genesis—Last Chapter.")

Admission (*in private*)   In these next moments, close your eyes and let come to you in a minute of silence your own contribution to pollution in the world . . . the tight shell of me . . . the cool enclosure of I . . . the carelessness of myself . . . the wasteful acts . . . litter on the highway . . . alcohol on my lips . . . filth in my mind . . . smoke in the room.

Public Trial *Confession for Misuse of Earth—Mock Trial form*
STRAIGHT MAN   Hear ye, hear ye, the district court of the Great

Chain of Being is now in session, the Honorable Divine Spirit, Judge of the Universe, presiding. The defendants at the bar have heard the appropriate sections from the statutes of the Book of Life. How do they plead?

ACCUSED   Your Honor, we enter a plea of Guilty in the Court of the Great Spirit:

> To first degree murder of redwoods,
> To grand larceny of grasslands,
> To statutory rape of minor woodlands,
> To unnatural acts of urban living,
> To willful arson of forests,
> To unwarranted seizure of rice crops,
> To mutilation of human form divine,
> To misappropriation of natural resources,
> To willful violation of the Pure Food and Drug Act,
> To genocide against herbivorous,
> To drunken driving across continents,
> To improper combustion of fossil fuels,
> To lewd and lascivious waterproofing of the earth,
> To unlawful possession of insecticides,
> To writing blank checks on the future,
> To unauthorized handling of fissionable materials,
> To illegal dumping of detergents,
> To illegal manufacturing of garbage,
> To trespassing on private property of animals,
> To murder of the air, water, earth, flora, fauna,
>   black men, red men, yellow men,
> To repeated public acts of self-abuse,
> We enter a plea of Guilty
> To constant adult delinquency.

DEFENSE ATTORNEY   We accept the penalty prescribed by the inflexible laws of nature, and we ask the God of all grace and nature to change our minds for the future.

The sad thing about us is that we are ruining our environment and ourselves and others . . . let us continue our prayer corporately:

PEOPLE

> Thank you, Father, for the chance to be confronted
> with the harm being done.
> Thank you for the chance to admit it to ourselves
> and to you.
> Forgive us if we cannot trust enough truly to be
> able to confess.
> Hear us with the compassion of Christ in whose
> Name we are forgiven. Amen [3]

Proclamation (*Psalm 148*) The Bible says:

> Praise the Lord!
> Praise the Lord from the heavens,
>   praise him in the heights!
> Praise him, all his angels,
>   praise him, all his host!
> Praise him, sun and moon,
>   praise him, all you shining stars!
>   vs. 1–3

LET'S SING (*seated*) "For the Beauty of the Earth" (*verse 1*).
The Bible says:

> Let them praise the name of the Lord!
>   For he commanded and they were created.
> And he established them for ever and ever;
>   he fixed their bounds which cannot be passed.
>   vs. 5, 6

LET'S SING (*verse 2*). The Bible says:

> Praise the Lord from the earth,
>   you sea monsters and all deeps,
> fire and hail, snow and frost,
>   stormy wind fulfilling his command!
>
> Mountains and all hills,
>   fruit trees and all cedars!
> Beasts and all cattle,
>   creeping things and flying birds!
>   vs. 7–10

LET'S SING (*verse 3*). The Bible says:

> Kings of the earth and all peoples,
>   princes and all rulers of the earth!
> Young men and maidens together,
>   old men and children!
>
> Let them praise the name of the Lord,
>   for his name alone is exalted. . . .
>   vs. 11–13

LET'S SING (*verse 4*). The Bible says:

> Praise the Lord!
> Praise God in his sanctuary;
>   praise him in his mighty firmament!
> Praise him for his mighty deeds;
>   praise him according to his exceeding greatness!
>
> Praise him with trumpet sound;
>   praise him with lute and harp!
> Praise him with timbrel and dance;
>   praise him with strings and pipe!
> Praise him with sounding cymbals;
>   praise him with loud clashing cymbals!
> Let everything that breathes praise the Lord!
> Praise the Lord!
>   Psalm 150

LET'S SING (*verse 5*)

The Life of The Church   What Your Church is Doing

The Giving of Gifts
PRAYER
A SONG OF FAITH (*choir*)   "Put Your Hand in the Hand of the Man"

The Word Spoken   "Recycling the Earth–Recycling People"
RESPONSE   The Christian's Credo (*standing*)
   I believe in God the Father Almighty, Maker of heaven and earth.

I believe that soil and water, air and forests, are as vast as the world—that they are the foundations of my past, the realities of my present, and the essentials of my future—but that they are not limitless.

I believe that they, with the human soul, represent the purity of nature, but are being polluted—that they are the gifts of God, but are being misused.

Therefore I affirm—the conservation of nature and the care of human lives—I affirm the cleansing of pollution on the planet, and the cleansing of sin in the soul.

Above all I believe in the coming on earth of Jesus Christ our Lord, in order that the world might be recycled through Him. Amen!

Blessing

LEADER   Go forth into a world where apathy and abuse are dominant. Move the world a little, in the name of the Father, the Son, and the Holy Spirit, and the Lord be with you.

PEOPLE   Lord, let us leave now filled anew with You, and pledged to Your service in all that we do.

Though we have some questions our faith in You is sure; we know You are with us and Your way will endure. Amen!

OUTDOOR PICNIC AND COMMUNION SERVICE [4]

Preparation: After the picnic, divide worshipers into groups of about eight people; each group sits together on a blanket; a HOST *is chosen for each group.*

Informal Hymn Singing

Call to Worship

LEADER   What are all of you people doing seated on the ground?

PEOPLE   We have gathered to hear and participate in the Word of God,

HOSTS   And, to praise God,

PEOPLE   And, to break bread together,

HOSTS   And, to express our love,

PEOPLE   And, to pray for others,

HOSTS   And, to pray for ourselves,

PEOPLE   And, to thank God for life.

LEADER   Then, let us come into His presence with singing.

HYMN OF ADORATION   "Now Thank We All Our God"

Confessional With Rice

LEADER   Within each group, pass the bowl of rice from person to person. Filter the rice through your hands and reflect on the difficulty we have in realizing the extent of universal human suffering. People are hurting by the hundreds of thousands—like so many grains of rice sifting through praying hands—yet we tend towards apathy because we cannot think of repression, death, hunger, and disease on a massive scale. As you meditate, each host will guide our confession of unconcern. (*Simultaneously* HOST *directs thoughts for his group's prayers; allow three minutes.*)

UNISON   The Lord's Prayer (*led by* LEADER).

Responsive Reading (1 Corinthians 13, *paraphrased*)

LEADER   You should set your hearts on the highest spiritual gifts, but I will show you what is the highest way of all. If I were to speak with the combined eloquence of men and angels I should stir men like a fanfare of trumpets or the crashing of cymbals, but unless I had love, I should do nothing more.

PEOPLE   If I cleverly combine all the current clichés so as to impress and confound my contemporaries, and have not love, they are but empty noises.

HOSTS   If I had the gift of foretelling the future and had in my mind not only human knowledge but the secrets of God, and if, in addition, I had absolute faith which can move mountains, but had no love, I tell you I should amount to nothing at all.

PEOPLE   If I master all scientific knowledge and conquer space
and explore planets, and if I can split atoms, but have not love,
my world shall be barren and desolate.

LEADER   If I were to sell all my possessions to feed the hungry,
and, for my convictions, allow my body to be burned, and yet
had no love, I should achieve precisely nothing.

PEOPLE   If I increase my pledge so there may be more on appor-
tionment and seek out new members and yet have no love, it is
nothing.

HOSTS   This love of which I speak is slow to lose patience. It
looks for a way of being constructive. It is not possessive, it is
neither anxious to impress nor does it cherish inflated ideas of
its own importance.

PEOPLE   These goodly works which I attempt must reflect love.
Love is not arrogant—love breaketh down barriers—counts not
the cost of involvement—never succumbs to the expedient.

LEADER   Love has good manners and does not pursue selfish ad-
vantage. It is not touchy. It does not compile statistics of evil
or gloat over the wickedness of other people. On the contrary,
it is glad with all good men when truth prevails.

PEOPLE   Love is composed and gentle, yet possesses an inner
strength and warmth. Love expresses a compassionate concern
for others.

HOSTS   Love knows no limits to its endurance, no end to its trust,
no fading of its hope. It can outlast anything. It is, in fact, the
one thing that still stands when all else has fallen.

PEOPLE   Love does the little tasks. Love's equilibrium is not dis-
turbed by the irksome; it is content with serving in an obscure
capacity but does not reject the challenge of heroic leadership.

ALL   In this life we have three great lasting qualities—faith,
hope, and love. But the greatest of them is love.[5]

Offertory

LEADER   We present now our offerings of love.

(*Each group will discuss tangible love for God led by the* HOST
*while the offering baskets are passed through the groups. Allow
five minutes.*)

HYMN "Doxology" (*With the* CONGREGATION *standing, the offering is presented.*)

Proclamation (INTERPRETERS *will present a visual adaption of Psalm 100 while the Psalm is being read.*)

CONGREGATIONAL RESPONSE (*The* CONGREGATION *will join with the* INTERPRETERS *in a second reading of Psalm 100.*)

Communion Scripture Luke 9:10–17 and John 61:1–15. (*The scriptural sections are to be read and discussed in the individual groups. Each* HOST *will guide the reading and reflecting.*)

Following are some questions to ponder:

(a) Why did Jesus test Philip and what response did He expect?

(b) Did the people understand the meaning of the miracle correctly?

(c) What do you believe is the overall meaning of these stories?

(d) How can food be stretched today?

(e) What was the meaning of the symbol of the twelve remaining baskets of food?

(f) Later in the same week, Jesus referred to Himself as the "bread of life." Do these two references to bread have anything in common?

(g) Why is bread such an important symbol of our faith?

(h) Is there any difference in these two stories about the feeding of the multitude and if so, why do you think they are different and what do the differences say?

The Communion (*One loaf of bread and one cup are placed on the altar. After the prayer of thanks and the invitation to communion, each group comes forward to partake, taking just as little as possible so that "the multitudes may be fed." After serving himself, each person in each of the groups will form into a large circle to receive the benediction.*)

COMMUNION MEDITATION

Man does not live by bread alone, but by the wonderful things such as beauty and harmony, truth and goodness, work and recreation, affection and friendship, aspiration and worship.

Not by bread alone, but by the beauty of the skies and the loveliness of the land and seas,

Not by bread alone, but by the creations of artists, the lyrics of poets, and the biographies of great men.

Not by bread alone, but by comradeship and high adventures, seeking and finding, serving and sharing, loving and being loved.

Man does not live by bread alone, but by being faithful in prayer, responding to the guidance of the Holy Spirit, finding and doing the loving will of God now and eternally.

Jesus said, "I am the [true] Bread of Life. No one coming to me will ever be hungry again. Those believing in me will never thirst" (John 6:35 LB).

THE THANKSGIVING PRAYER   All praise be to You, O God, our Father, for the life and spirit of Jesus Christ, who so loved that He gave Himself for others, even when it meant death. May these symbols of His sacrifice feed us as spiritual food, that we may become like Him in spirit in all that we do. Amen.

THE INVITATION   You who discern in these emblems the broken body and shed blood of Jesus, and desire to live for Him, come now, take, eat, and drink, and assimilate Him more fully into your being.

(*After the partaking form closing circle.*)

THE BENEDICTION (*by the* LEADER)   May grace and peace be multiplied in your lives, through the knowledge of God and of Jesus our Lord. Amen.

HYMN   "Blest Be the Tie That Binds"

WORSHIP IN A MOUNTAIN SETTING

Hymn Sing
"For the Beauty of the Earth"
"This Is My Father's World"

"Climb Every Mountain"
"He's Got the Whole World in His Hands"

Call to Worship

> I lift up my eyes to the hills
> From whence does my help come?
> My help comes from the Lord,
> Who made heaven and earth.
> Psalm 121:1, 2

PRAYER   O God of the Universe that we see and all that we do not see: We are glad for mountains that lift us above the level of the plains.

For their heights that lead the eye and the soul to the summits of thought and purpose; for the clouds that wreathe them in mystery; for the morning sun that touches them with glory; for their strong shelter through the silent nights—we give thanks.

O God of Human Life—set mountains for us to climb—a mighty purpose for which to live; vast and selfless ambitions; services to render and reforms to accomplish; character goals that challenge. Grant to us, O God, sunlight to brighten our valleys and to glorify the days. Let the peaks tower above the low levels of life and draw all smaller things to the redeeming touch of greatness as we see it in the peak of all peaks, Jesus the Christ. Amen.

HYMN   "Spirit of the Living God, Fall Afresh on Me"

THE WORD FROM THE PSALMIST   (*Choose from among these: Psalm 139; 121; 19:1–6; 29; 24:3, 4.*)

The Poet

> "On the Heights"
> Within the shelter of the hills
> God is so near!
> I feel the closeness of One
> Who often left the weary crowd
> That touched His garment's hem

And went for strength to where
The silent hills could comfort
His breaking heart,
And lift a burden too great
To be borne alone.

I stand in the early morning's light
With all around the sound of wings invisible,
Hearing, knowing, feeling things
That never leave the heights sublime.
Like Moses, I might see
A great white flame
In this still sacred place,
Then like him, I hide my face
And breathe the Master's holy name.[6]

"Bring Me Men"

Bring me men to match my mountains,
    Bring me men to match my plains—
Men with empires in their purpose
    And new eras in their brains.
Bring me men to match my prairies,
    Men to match my inland seas,
Men whose thought shall prove a highway
    Up to ampler destinies,
Pioneers to clear thought's marshlands
    And to cleanse old error's fen;
Bring me men to match my mountains—
    Bring me men!

Bring me men to match my forests,
    Strong to fight the storm and blast,
Branching toward the skyey future,
    Rooted in the fertile past.
Bring me men to match my valleys,
    Tolerant of sun and snow,
Men within whose fruitful purpose
    Time's consummate blooms shall grow,
Men to tame the tigerish instincts
    Of the lair and cave and den,

Cleanse the dragon slime of nature—
Bring me men!

Bring me men to match my rivers,
Continent cleavers, flowing free,
Drawn by the eternal madness
To be mingled with the sea;
Men of oceanic impulse,
Men whose moral currents sweep
Towards the wide-infolding ocean
Of an undiscovered deep;
Men who feel the strong pulsation
Of the Central Sea, and then
Time their currents to its earth throb—
Bring me men! [7]

SOLO "God Who Touches Earth with Beauty"

Sermon "Climbing Spiritual Mountains" or "God is Speaking—How?"

HYMN "God of the Mountain"

CAMPFIRE SERVICE

Singspiration (*Someone with guitar leads the singing if possible.*) "Edges of His Ways," "There Must Be a God Somewhere," "Whisper a Prayer," "Kumbaya," "Pass It On," "Spirit of the Living God"

POEM

Twilight in the Foothills
Twilight in the foothills
Deep'ning into dark.

Far away the nocturne
Of a meadow lark.

Purple, wooded hill slopes
Fading out of sight.
Unseen hands are drawing
The tapestries of night.

Shadowy forms come creeping
Forth from hidden lairs.
Pines with arms uplifted
Offer evening prayers.

Soft lights smile a welcome
To homeward bound,
Where, when tasks are ended,
Rest and love are found.[8]

Scripture Sentences About Nature

The heavens are telling the glory of God;
   and the firmament proclaims his handiwork.
                           Psalm 19:1

Thine is the day, thine also the night;
   thou hast established the luminaries and the sun.
Thou hast fixed all the bounds of the earth;
   thou hast made summer and winter.
                         Psalm 74:16, 17

PRAYER OF PRAISE   I am asking you to join me in a prayer that was written nearly seven hundred and fifty years ago by a man in Assisi, Italy, called Francis who knew much about our world. He referred to ants and other creatures, as well as the planets, as "brother," "sister." They are essential fellow-planet riders on whom we depend, and with whom, in God's mysterious grace, this whirling earth is saved from being empty like the moon. As I read the words of St. Francis, let us pray, with our eyes focused on a star.

Praise be my Lord God with all His creatures and especially our brother the sun, who brings us the day and who brings us light; fair is he and shines with a very great splendor. O Lord, he shows us You.

Praise be my Lord for our sister the moon, and for the stars, which He has set clear and lovely in the heavens.

Praise be my Lord for our brother the wind, and for air and cloud, calms, and all weather by which You uphold life in all creatures.

Praise be my Lord for our sister water, who is very serviceable unto us, and humble and precious and clean.

Praise be my Lord for our brother fire, through whom You give us light in the darkness; and he is bright and pleasant and very strong.

Praise be my Lord for our mother the earth, who sustains us and keeps us and brings forth diverse fruits and flowers of many colors, and grass.

Praise be my Lord for all those who pardon one another for His love's sake, and who endure weakness and tribulation. Blessed are they who peaceably shall endure.

Praise be my Lord for our sister the death of the body, from which no man escapes. Blessed are those who are found walking by Your most holy will.

Praise and bless the Lord; and give thanks to Him; and serve Him with great humility.

SONG   "A New Tomorrow"

Scripture   (*Choose from Psalm 139, 8, 121; Job 26:7, 9, 10, 12, 14.*)
SOLO   "How Great Thou Art"

Thoughts in the Night   (*suggested homilies*)
   "The Greatness of God" (*homily on Psalm 139*) or
   "He Made the Stars Also" (*homily on Genesis 1:16*) or
   "God is Speaking (*homily on Psalm 29*)
SILENCE (*while watching the stars*)

Conclusion
ALL   "Taps"

> Day is done,
> Gone the sun,

From the lake,
From the hill,
From the sky,
All is well;
Safely rest.
God is nigh.

GUIDED RETREAT OF SILENCE

A twenty-six-hour retreat into silence may take place in a secluded area of nature, preferably a campsite in the mountains or overlooking a lake. The retreat begins with a worship service during which time explanations are made as to procedures, facilities, schedule, resource literature, and directed thoughts for meditation. There is no talking following the opening service until the breaking of the silence with the Doxology. An office room should be assigned for handling emergencies. The schedule should be as relaxed and unstructured as possible, yet with sufficient directions to give meaning to the experience. Pencil and tablet, Bible and devotional literature, and a flashlight should be brought by each worshiper.

SCHEDULE

First Day
6:00 P.M.   DINNER, FUN, AND FELLOWSHIP
7:00 P.M.   ORIENTATION
7:30 P.M.   WORSHIP SERVICE
SONGS   "Spirit of the Living God," "Day is Dying in the West,"
   "God Who Touchest Earth with Beauty"

SOLO "Immortal, Invisible, God Only Wise"

SCRIPTURE 139th Psalm

PRAYER Let us pray in the words of W. E. Orchard: "O God—come to us through the silence in the night, or meet us in the desert, or if we shun the lonely way, meet us in the crowd—but speak above the tumult in thunder to our souls. Amen."

Meditation "The Majesty of Silence" When one reads the devotional sections of the Bible, how often he is confronted with an invitation to the "Majesty of Silence." "Be still, and know that I am God . . . in quietness and in trust shall be your strength . . . they who wait for the Lord shall renew their strength; they shall mount up with wings like eagles, they shall run and not be weary; they shall walk and not faint. . . ." When one reads the biographical materials of the Biblical giants, he is aware of the place of mystical quietness. Moses became convinced of God and His will in the solitude of a lonely desert. Elijah found God not in the tempest or earthquake or fire but "after the fire a still small voice." Remember how often Jesus went into the quiet places—sometimes to spend the entire night. To His disciples He said, "Come away by yourselves to a lonely place, and rest a while. . . ."

In fact the poet, in contrast to the sensationalism, noisy fanfares, and blinding signs announcing modern coming events, describes the Incarnation in these words:

> How silently, how silently
> The wondrous gift is [was] given!
> So God imparts to human hearts
> The blessings of His heaven.[9]

One is also impressed with the fact that the persons who have climbed the tallest peaks of spiritual experience, both in the past and today, are those who have disciplined times of silence.

Therefore, let us consider briefly why silence is important; when it is advisable to be silent, and how to use silence creatively.

First, *why is silence important?*

There are three reasons. It is a practical necessity, a psychological necessity, and a theological necessity.

Pentecost is a day of great significance to the church. It was the day the Holy Spirit descended with power upon the disciples, giving them ability to witness. It was the day the Apostle Peter gave the keys for unlocking the Kingdom. It was the day three thousand souls were baptized into Christ, and hence His church was born.

But note—this spiritual happening was preceded by forty days of solitude and quiet. After the Ascension of our Lord, the disciples were commanded to tarry in Jerusalem, until they were clothed with power from on high. They went to the Upper Room, which was an island of solitude midst the agitation of a thriving, busy, crowded city—and there devoted themselves to prayer. "You shall receive power," they were promised, "when the Holy Spirit has come upon you, and you shall be my witnesses. . . ."

Ah, mighty works must be preceded by silent preparation. Meaningful activity is dependent upon insight. Periods of reflection are needed if confused action is to be avoided.

The modern church has lost this power—not because of poor equipment, or intellectual ignorance—but because we have not spent enough time in solitude to receive the Holy Spirit.

Our individual lives are impoverished with shallowness and superficiality and exhaustion, because the unconscious mental energies which give us power have not been replenished at the fountain of solitude.

Likewise, silence is a *psychological necessity*. Nervous disorders, heart disease, mental breakdowns, ulcers are becoming apparently more commonplace. We Americans are speed-minded and find our greatest satisfaction in action. We are restless, the tempo of life is becoming swifter and swifter, and the stress and strain is showing. The struggle for livelihood and the pressure for success are leading us to states of frenzy—tying us in knots which we cannot untie—making us irritable and emotionally upset. Much of our sickness is psychological.

This generation desperately needs to slow down and be patient and quiet. The psychological wounds caused by frantic living can be healed by the inner unity derived from harmony with God.

Many reputable psychologists and psychiatrists agree that the Christian religion is a vital influence for producing that confidence of soul and harmonious stability that such a large proportion of our society needs. This is why the communion service each Sunday is mental therapy. "In quietness and confidence shall be your strength . . . they that wait upon the Lord shall renew their strength . . . the Lord is my Shepherd, He restoreth my soul."

> Drop Thy still dews of quietness,
> Till all our strivings close;
> Take from our souls the strain and stress,
> And let our ordered lives confess
> The beauty of Thy peace.[10]

Then silence, above all, is a *theological necessity*. He who would know God intimately and commune with Him must discipline himself to silence. C. H. Dodd in his commentary on Romans said, "Faith is an act which is the negation of all activity, a moment of passivity out of which the strength for action comes, because in it God acts." Religion begins as an essential mystic experience. "Be still and know that I am God." It begins with a negation to all activity. Our fussy activities must halt if God and the overworld would become real to us; otherwise, only the passing pageantry of things in which we spend so much time is real. The reason God is not more real to some is because they do not spend time with Him. We live so much on the surface and exterior of our life that the mysterious inwardness of our souls is not real.

Accustomed to talking with everyone and anyone, and having the TV or radio blaring all day long, we cannot hear the still small voice that speaks to our conscience. Our ear is not attuned adequately to the way God communicates, for He can only be heard in stillness.

Even in our religious habits, silence is embarrassing or difficult.

Our mind wanders. In our prayers, we do the talking, when we should also be listening. At worship if no one is speaking, the organ isn't playing, or the choir is not singing, we assume that nothing is happening.

> Oh world, invisible—I view thee
> Oh world intangible—I touch thee
> Oh world unknowable—I know thee.
> Inapprehensible—I clutch thee.[11]

8:15 P.M.   BEGIN CREATIVE SILENT VIGIL
8:30–11:00   (*Separate, to some outdoor beauty spot.*)
- Read Genesis 1; Psalm 121; Psalm 8 and other Scriptures as selected (*need flashlight and Bible*)
- MEDITATION "Under the Stars"
  1 Find as many constellations as possible.
  2 Count the stars in a specific area.
  3 Think about the statement, "He made the stars also."
  4 "What is man, that God is mindful of him."
- PRAYER—Directed Thoughts
  1 For a "Closer Walk With God."
  2 Confess with sorrow, the conditions on earth that grieve God.
  3 Confess our sins of omission and commission.
- LISTENING
- RETIRING
11:00 P.M.   LIGHTS OUT
Second Day
7:00 A.M.   RISING
7:30 A.M.   NATURE WALK
- Tabulate the sounds you hear.
- Tabulate the different kinds of birds, insects, animals you see.
- Pick different leaves, flowers you see.
- Think about the beauty, order, and blessings of nature.
8:15 A.M.   BREAKFAST AND CLEAN-UP
9:15 A.M.   STUDY AND MEDITATION TIME
- Read from available devotional literature:

Frank Laubach, "Prayer"; Thomas Kepler, "Journey With the Saints"; George A. Buttrick, "Prayer"; Elton Trueblood, "The Company of the Committed"; Albert E. Day, "An Autobiography of Prayer"
- Read from the Bible:
  Psalm 29; Psalm 23; Amos 2; 4; Hebrews 1
- Can you hear God speaking
  —in nature? What is He saying to me?
  —in world happenings? What is He saying to me?
  —in your church? What is He saying to me?
  —in the Bible? What is He saying to me?
  —in Jesus? What is He saying to me?
- Write a paragraph on "What I Hear God Saying to Our World Today"

10:30 A.M. SILENT GROUP ACTIVITY
- Recreation—swimming, hiking, baseball, etc.
- Inside Games (*see suggestions below*):

Inside Games

TIT-TAT-TOE (*Group divided into two groups. Large "Tit-Tat-Toe" chalked on floor. Teams alternate with persons stepping into squares to attempt three team members in a row, or to block opponents from doing same. No words need to be spoken. After fifteen games, the winner is determined.*)

CARD GAME ("Hearts" *can be played without speaking*)

WRITING GAMES (*Mimeograph and circulate quizzes. After sufficient time, a correct list can be posted or written on blackboard.*) [12]

12:00 NOON LUNCH

1:00 P.M. CREATIVE WRITING—of feelings—in poetry, short story, parable, or paraphrasing Scriptures.

2:30 P.M. REST

4:00 P.M. PRIVATE GOALING
- Write "The Kind of Person I Want to Become"; "Ten Ways I Want to Improve"; "Habits I Need to Overcome"; or "Specific Resolves I Make."

5:00 P.M. COMMUNION SERVICE (*in the woods . . . by lake shore . . . vesper area . . . Total group is seated. Then teams of two go to the table spread with a loaf and cup. Each gestures gratitude, penitence, concern, prayer. Then each serves the other, symbolic of sharing life. When finished, a friendship circle is formed. When the* LEADER *gives the signal,* The Doxology *is sung, officially breaking the silence.*)

5:30 P.M. FELLOWSHIP TIME (*While visiting, discuss* "What This Retreat Has Meant to Me.")

6:00 P.M. DINNER

7:00 P.M. CONCLUDING PRAYER

        SONG "Blest Be the Tie That Binds"

SOURCE NOTES

Section 1 DEVELOPING THE CONTEMPORARY ATMOSPHERE

1. James F. White, *New Forms of Worship*, p. 104.

Section 2 CELEBRATIVE ENCOUNTERS

1. By Mary Lou Lacy, *And God Wants People*.

2. By Darrell Faires, *Songs N' Celebrae*, p. 2.

3. By Peter Scholtes, *Hymnal for Young Christians*.

4. From Isthmanian Youth Fellowship, Union Christian Church, Canal Zone, Panama, and used by other groups. Original author unknown.

5. Service by Jon A. Lacey used in Chapman College People's Church, Orange, California, February 13, 1972.

6. Youth Service, First Christian Church, Winfield, Kansas, July 30, 1972. Orvan Gilstrap, Minister.

7. By Robert Raines

8. By Samuel Pugh in *World Call*, March 1972, p. 46.

9. By Malcolm Boyd, *Are You Running With Me, Jesus?* p. 43.

10. By Norman C. Habel, *Interrobang*, p. 15.

11. By Darrell Faires, *Songs N' Celebrae*, p. 11.

12. There are numerous editions of this work.

13. This speech was given at the Freedom March on Washington, August 28, 1963.

14. Adapted from Service of Church Women United of Kansas, April 6, 1970.

15. "Neighbors," Produced by the National Film Board of Canada, 1952, from *Discovery in Film*, Paulist Press, Paramus, N.J., p. 139. Slides should be local ones if possible. Environmental groups may have films or slides available.

16. By Ruth Johnston Hulse.

17. By Jack Walker, *An Oracle*, First Christian Church, Reseda, California.

18. By Arthur Waskow, *The Freedom Seder*.

19. Adaptation by Jack Fascinato and Ernest J. Ford. © 1960 Snyder Music Corporation.

20. By Warren Lane Moulton, Public Domain.

21. Author Unknown.

22. Adapted from Worship Service, Downey Avenue Christian Church, Indianapolis, Indiana, August 1, 1971.

23. From the Unified Promotion Folder, *The Christian Church*, Indianapolis, Indiana.

24. Suggested readings from *The Treasure Chest*, Harper & Row, Publishers: "Eternal Joy" by Paul Tillich (p. 155), "True Joy" by George Bernard Shaw (p. 155), "Unexpected Surprises" by Samuel Longfellow (p. 155), "Christianity" by Hugh Elmer Brown (p. 156).

25. Originally arranged by Chaplain Robert Geller, United Campus Minister, Colorado State University, Fort Collins, Colorado. Used in Danforth Chapel, May 31, 1971.

Section 3 FESTIVAL OCCASIONS

1. Developed over the years by James L. Christensen.

2. By Roy M. Pearson, *The Christian Century*, December 17, 1952, p. 1466.

3. Adapted from the scroll in The Garden at Clifton, Los Angeles, California. Copyright 1955 by the Christian Board of Publication. Used by permission.

4. By Harold G. Roberts, *Ventures in Worship*, edited by David James Randolph, p. 48.

5. Adapted from *The Book of Worship for Church and Home*, p. 46.

6. Originated by Robert T. Cooke, United Presbyterian Church, Whitinsville, Mass.

7. The hymns used here are all in public domain and may be found in most hymn books.

8. By Norman Habel, *Interrobang*, page 82.

9. *Ibid.*, p. 70.

10. *New Hymnbook for Christian Worship*, Christian Board of Publication, St. Louis, Mo., p. 490.

11. James L. Christensen, *The Complete Funeral Manual*, pp. 98, 99.

12. Service used at Calvary United Methodist Church, Nashville, Tennessee.

12a. From *More Contemporary Prayers* by Caryl Micklem.

13. By Raymond Gaylord, *World Call*, March, 1972.

14. From Calvary United Methodist Church, Nashville, Tenn.

15. Service used at Grace United Methodist Church, Donald Barnes, minister, Kokomo, Indiana.

16. This filmstrip (or photovisuals) may be obtained from Pflaum/ Standard, 38 W. 5th Street, Dayton, Ohio, 45402.

Section 4 WEDDING CELEBRATIONS

1. Prepared by Barbara Baird and Mike Myers for their wedding, August 10, 1972, Fort Worth, Texas.

2. Planned for wedding of Dorothy Claire Caccamo and H. Larry Humm of Wappingers Falls, New York.

3. Prepared by the Reverend James R. Monroe for his marriage to Mary Catherine Inglefield, July 15, 1966, Arlington, Texas.

4. Adapted from "The New Rite of Marriage" by the International Committee on English in the Liturgy, Inc., 1969, and "Together for Life" by Joseph M. Champlin (Notre Dame, Indiana: Ave Maria Press, 1970).

Section 5 SMALL GROUP EXPERIMENTS

1. James L. Christensen, *The Complete Funeral Manual*, pp. 43, 44.

2. From *The Weekly*, Edited by Dr. Ray Montgomery, Speedway Christian Church, Indianapolis, Indiana.

3. By Mamie Jean Cole, from *The Treasure Chest*, Charles L. Wallis, editor.

4. By John Henry Jowett, *The Treasure Chest*.

5. From *The Treasure Chest*.

6. *Ibid.*

7. *Ibid.*

8. *Ibid.*

Section 6 OUTDOOR WORSHIP OCCASIONS

1. Adapted from Youth Service, Raleigh Presbyterian Church, Memphis, Tennessee, January 30, 1972.

2. Written by Kenneth Ross while a student in Upper Moreland (Pa.) High School. Included in *The Conservationist*, June–July, 1971,

p. 33, published by the State of New York, Department of Environmental Conservation, Albany, N.Y.

3. By Jack W. Lundin, *Liturgies for Life*, pp. 133, 134.

4. Adapted from Worship Service, at Calvary United Methodist Church, Nashville, Tennessee.

5. *Ibid.*

6. By Jane Warren Vivian, *Worship Highways*, p. 184.

7. By Sam Walter Foss, Public Domain.

8. By Chester Larue Hampton, *Worship Highways*, p. 186.

9. "O Little Town of Bethlehem" verse 3.

10. "Dear Lord and Father of Mankind" verse 4, by John Greenleaf Whittier.

11. By Francis Thompson, "In No Strange Land," *Christ in Poetry,* Edited by Thomas and Hazel Clark.

12. There are a number of fine books available for quiet games. *See* E. O. Harbin's *The Fun Encyclopedia*, published by Abingdon Press. For Bible quizzes *see* Carl S. Shoup's *Test Your Bible Knowledge,* published by Fleming H. Revell Company.

INDEX OF SONGS AND THEIR SOURCES

The following songs are suggestions for services in this book. Many of them have been recorded by more than one artist and no effort has been made to select the best recording. Some of these songs can be found in sheet music as well as on records or tapes. Hymns indicated as being in public domain or "traditional" may be found in a wide variety of hymnals. For additional music sources see CONTEMPORARY WORSHIP SERVICES by James L. Christensen, published by Fleming H. Revell Company.

BIBLIOGRAPHY AND RESOURCES

Anderson, Robert W. and Caemerer, Richard R. *Banners, Banners, Banners.* Chicago: Christian Art Associates, 1967.

Anderson, Vienna, *Create and Celebrate.* New York: Morehouse-Barlow Co., Inc., 1972.

Banyard, Edmund, ed. 1969. *Word Alive.* London: Belton Books.

Bimbler, Richard 1972. *Pray, Praise and Hooray.* St. Louis, Missouri: Concordia Publishing House.

Bloy, Myron B., Jr., ed. 1969. *Multi-Media Worship.* New York: Seabury Press.

Book of Common Worship Provisional Services, The. Philadelphia: Westminster Press, 1966.

Brown, John P., and York, Richard L. (compilers). *The Covenant of Peace: A Liberation Prayer Book.* New York: Morehouse-Barlow Co., Inc.

Bush, Roger 1971. *Hey! J. C.!.* Dayton, Ohio: Pflaum, Standard.

Champlin, Joseph M. 1970. *Together For Life.* Notre Dame, Indiana: Ave Maria Press.

Christensen, James L. 1970. *Contemporary Worship Services.* Old Tappan, N.J.: Fleming H. Revell Company.

Faires, Darrell 1972. *Songs 'N Celebrae.* St. Louis, Missouri: Shalom Publications.

Galen, John (Editor). *Eucharistic Liturgies.* Produced by the (Roman Catholic) Woodstock Center for Religion and Worship, 475 Riverside Drive, New York, 10027.

Gelineau, Joseph. *Psalms: A Singing Version.* Paramus, N.J.: Paulist/Newman Press.

Good News For Modern Man. New York: American Bible Society, 1966.

Groenfeldt, John S. *The Church Faces Issues—Worship.* CLC Press. Part of the Covenant Life curriculum and an adult study book for the Presbyterian Church, U.S.

217

218   NEW WAYS TO WORSHIP

Hoon, Paul W. *The Integrity of Worship*. Nashville: Abingdon Press.

Hovda, Robert and Huck, Gabe 1971. *There's No Place Like People*. Chicago: Argus Communications.

Hymns For Now, Vols. I, II and III. St. Louis: Concordia Publishing House.

Kirby, J., ed. 1969. *Word and Action: New Forms of Liturgy*. New York: Seabury Press.

It Doesn't Have To Be With Guitars. DeWitt, New York: Pebble Hill Presbyterian Church, 1971.

Jerusalem Bible. New York: Doubleday & Company, Inc., 1966.

Jurack, Simone. *How Is A Banner*. Chicago: Christian Art Associates.

Link, Mark, S.J. 1971. *He Is the Still Point of the Turning World*. Chicago: Argus Communications.

Lundin, Jack W. 1972. *Liturgies For Life*. Downers Grove, Illinois: C.C.S. Publishing House.

Manual of Celebration. The (Roman Catholic) Liturgical Conference, Inc., 1330 Massachusetts Ave., N.W., Washington, D.C. 20005

Mass Media Ministries. 2116 No. Charles St., Baltimore, Maryland 21218. A biweekly newsletter, which analyzes and critiques current films, television, books, recordings and other audio-visual productions.

Micklem, Caryl, ed. 1970. *More Contemporary Prayers*. London: S.C.M. Press, Ltd.

New Music and Arts Exchange, The. 152 West 66th Street, New York, 10023. A full catalog to facilitate the process of exchange of new materials between radical and experimental artists and other creative persons or groups.

Odell, Garner Scott 1971. *The Church at Worship in an Urban Age*. Oakland, California: Celebration West.

Pebble Hill Presbyterian Church 1971. *It Doesn't Have To Be With Guitars*. DeWitt, N.Y.

Proclamation Productions, Inc., Orange Square, Port Jervis, New York, 12771. All kinds of musical and liturgical songs and ceremonies on the "mod" side.

Randolph, David James 1970. *Ventures In Worship Two*. Nashville, Tennessee: Abingdon.

SCAN, P. O. Box 12811, Pittsburgh, Pennsylvania 15241. A bimonthly bibliography of liturgical, musical, artists and audio-visual materials, including reviews.

Snyder, Ross 1971. *Contemporary Celebration.* Nashville, Tennessee: Abingdon.

TRAV (Television, Radio and Audio-Visuals), 341 Ponce de Leon Ave., N.E., Atlanta, Georgia 30308. Excellent bibliographical and technical help.

Time For Singing, A. (Geneva Press, 1970).

Thompson, Bard (Editor). *Liturgies of the Western Church.* Meridian Books, The World Publishing Company, 1961.

United Presbyterian Church in U.S.A., The 1966. *The Book of Common Worship: Provisional Services.* Philadelphia: Westminster Press.

White, James F. 1971. *New Forms of Worship.* Nashville, Tennessee: Abingdon.

Word and Action, New Forms of Liturgy. New York: Seabury Press, 1969.

Worship (Order of St. Benedict, Collegeville, Minn. 56321). A monthly review concerned with the problems of liturgical renewal.

Worshipbook, The—Services and Hymns. Philadelphia: Westminster Press, 1972.

Young, Carlton R. (Editor). *Songbook for Saints and Sinners.* Chicago: Agape.

INDEX

221